The Complete Beginners Guide to

Swimming

professional guidance and support to help you through every stage of learning how to swim

Mark Young

A Catalogue record for this book is available from the British Library

ISBN 9780992742898

Published by: Educate & Learn Publishing, Hertfordshire, UK

Graphics by Mark Young, courtesy of Poser V6.0

Design and typeset by Mark Young

Published in association with www.swim-teach.com

Warning: This book is intended for guidance and support only. Beginners and non-swimmers must NEVER enter a pool alone, unaided or without appropriate assistance. Neither the author nor the publisher can accept responsibility for any injury or loss sustained as a result of the use of this material.

Contents

Chapter 1: The Benefits of Swimming

Swimming: What's in it for you?

Swimming is an essential life skill and the benefits of swimming for all of us are huge, whatever our age, shape or size.

Research has proven over the years that the all over body workout we get from swimming has some major benefits on the human body and its various systems.

Discover some of the benefits to you that could prove to be life changing...

Your Heart and Lungs

Do you get out of breath doing normal everyday stuff? Regular swimming, once or twice a week will help to improve your stamina and overall fitness by getting your heart and lungs to do some work. Do not be put off my the word work or exercise because a swim only has to be gentle and of low intensity to still do wonders to your cardiovascular system.

Muscular Strength

We need muscular strength for all of our everyday activities, from walking around to getting up off of the couch. Swimming benefits all ages when it comes to strength and tone of our muscles.   Half an hour of swimming a couple of times a week and you will see the benefits in your toned muscles and you will feel stronger in yourself.

Flexibility of Your Joints

Regular swimming gets your muscles and bones moving and that in turn opens up and gets your joints moving nicely.   Moving your arms and legs in ways they are perhaps not used to or in ways they otherwise would not if they were not swimming, allows the joints in between them to stay supple and free-moving.

Improved Body Shape

Exercise in general gives us all that feel good factor, but swimming really has a positive effect on overall body shape. Regular swimming burns fat (the wobbly stuff under your skin, incase you didn't know!) and when that reduces and the muscles under the fat become toned and firm, the result: a fitter and more satisfying body shape.

Injury Rehabilitation

Regular swimming can have dramatic effects on injuries. The impact free nature of swimming allows muscles and joints to work and exercise but under conditions that are stress free and therefore promote the healing and rehabilitation of muscle pulls and joints strains. This is one of the key benefits of swimming.

Weight Loss

Like any other form of exercise, swimming burns calories and plenty of them. Because swimming is an all over body workout - in other words your whole body is continually moving as you swim - the net amount of calories is usually larger than that of other common forms of exercise.

Relieve Stress and Tension

There is nothing like escaping the stresses and tensions of life at the end of the working day. Whatever your job, be it a high-powered company director or a busy parent at home, you need time out to unwind and relax. Swimming offers just that: the chance to escape, relax and chill out. Let your mind wander away whilst you cruise up and down the pool at your own pace. And you get all the health and fitness benefits thrown in for good measure. Just what the doctor ordered!

Got a Back Problem?

Are you one of millions with a back problem? A lower back problem more than likely as this is the most common one. The zero impact nature of swimming allows your lower back and surrounding joints to move freely without the impact of the ground and your own body weight pressing through them constantly. It might not be a miracle cure but gentle impact free movements of swimming will all help, guaranteed.

Swimming During Pregnancy

It is a well-known fact that swimming while pregnant is safe and very beneficial to you and your unborn baby. The zero impact nature of swimming means there is no impact on your most load baring joints like the hips and knees. There is also no sudden jolting or bouncing movements to unsettle baby. So if you are pregnant swim all you like.

Post Surgery

Obviously it is important to consult your doctor about going swimming following an operation, as some people may have to wait a few weeks or months to avoid infection. Nonetheless, when the body is ready to be immersed into the water once gain, swimming can help to exercise the many major muscle groups, which can speed up the recovery process.

The Best Benefit of All - Fun and Enjoyment!

The benefits of swimming are numerous and people swim for various other reasons. To help with stress and health as well as cardiovascular fitness, right up to training and competitions, such as triathlons.

Most of us, particularly children, swim for fun. With fun comes health and fitness in the form of exercise and activity and most swimming pools and leisure facilities are in local areas and are relatively inexpensive.

Real Questions

"Is it too late to learn to swim? I never had the opportunity to learn to swim. I am an active senior citizen now. Can you give me some pointers on swimming for senior citizens?"

Mark's answer:

"It is never too late to learn to swim!

As for where to start, that all depends on how comfortable or uncomfortable you are in the water and in a swimming pool environment.

Find a swimming pool that is quiet and not full of children jumping all over the place. Most pools have their quiet times and busy times, so pick a time that is nice and quiet. Middle of the day when the kids are in school is usually best.

If you are a complete non-swimmer then take a friend or relative with you for help and support, from a safety point of view if nothing else.

If you have never been in a swimming pool before then your first step is to become relaxed and at ease in water of just below shoulder depth. Walking around, bobbing up and down, getting your face wet and partially submerging are all ways of getting used to the water and getting used to how your body behaves in the water.

If you are already comfortable in the water then lifting your feet off the bottom and taking the plunge is the next step. You may wish to use some goggles to prevent water getting in your eyes.

The easiest swimming stroke to learn as an adult beginner is breaststroke. Swimming breaststroke allows you to swim with your face out of the water and your head above the water surface. The arm and leg actions occur under the water and this makes the whole stroke easier and less tiring.

Use a swim noodle to give you some extra buoyancy and to help you get used to the arm and leg movements.

Do not be put off if you begin to get tired and out of breath. Your body is learning a brand new skill and exercising in a brand new way, so you are bound to get tired. For this reason it is important to take things one step at a time and do not overdo it.

When you walk out onto the poolside to get into the pool do not be embarrassed. Many adults are embarrassed at the fact they cannot swim and therefore shy away from trying. So, give yourself a pat on the back for having a go at learning something that many adults wish they could.

Get in the water, get on with it and enjoy yourself!"

"Which swimming stroke is good for my back? I always use breaststroke but understand front crawl is better for my lower back. I try front crawl but my legs ache and I cannot get far. I am 70yrs old and have swum since 6yrs old. Do you think I need lessons?"

Mark's answer:

"Front crawl is not the only swimming stroke that will take pressure away from your lower back. In fact there are a few ways of swimming that will help compliment your breaststroke.

Before you go spending money on swimming lessons try some of the following suggestions.

Swimming on your back is a great alternative to breaststroke and is better for the lower back. You do not have to swim full stroke backstroke, using the arms and all that. You could just swim on your back with your arms by your sides, using your hands to gently paddle under the water. If you are still unsure then using a float or a swim noodle under your arms will help give you confidence.

Many people make the mistake of kicking too much when swimming front crawl and the result is your aching tired legs. The majority of propulsion for front crawl comes from the arm action and even that does not have to be fast.

Try your front crawl placing less emphasis on the leg kick and more on the arms, but perform the stroke slowly. You may find you will go further without really trying.

You can also try swimming breaststroke but placing less emphasis on the leg kick. Although this is technically incorrect, the fact that you are swimming and doing some exercise is more important. The goal here is to keep fit, not to qualify for the Olympics.

Breaststroke can place pressure on the lower back in two ways. Firstly the powerful whip action leg kick places a slight impact and compression on the lower spine. Secondly the body position is at a slight angle rather than flat like front crawl and backstroke, which places an unnatural arch at the lower back.

Both of these can be adjusted to take some of the pressure away from the lower back. Firstly kick with less power and use your arms more, as mentioned already. Secondly make your body position flatter in the water by swimming with your chin lower in the water (maybe even face down) and extend your legs out further and higher behind you.

You do not have to eliminate breaststroke completely from your swimming. Maybe just reduce the amount of breaststroke you swim and replace some of your lengths with some of my suggestions above."

Chapter 2: Fear of Swimming

Is There Something Holding You Back?

Is your fear of swimming holding you back and preventing you from learning how to swim? Maybe it stops you from going anywhere near the swimming pool at all?

Maybe it is deep water that scares the life out of you because you think it will pull you down. Time to help calm your nerves.

Why do we have a fear of water?

The most common reason for having any kind of anxiety when it comes to getting in the swimming pool is usually linked to a bad experience in the past. This could have been a terrifying swimming lesson, an accidental fall into deep water or even a near drowning.

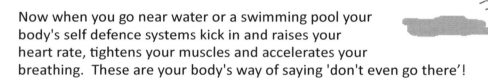

Now when you go near water or a swimming pool your body's self defence systems kick in and raises your heart rate, tightens your muscles and accelerates your breathing. These are your body's way of saying 'don't even go there'!

You might not have quite such a fear. Instead you could be one of those swimmers who swim happily around in the water until suddenly out of nowhere you feel like you're going to sink. You are swimming in deep water and it is going to pull you down and you instantly find yourself scrambling for the side to hold on to.

Ok, so how do you conquer your fear of swimming?

The short answer: slowly and gradually, step by step.

Step 1: learn how to hold your breath and to breathe out into the water. Yes, blow bubbles! Human beings cannot breathe underwater (sorry to state the obvious here), so we have to learn to control our breathing whilst in the water. If we control our breathing, then our heart rate will be lower, our muscles will be less tense and overall we will become more relaxed.

Try standing in water of about chest or shoulder depth, take a deep breath and partially submerge your face into the water. Allow your mouth and nose to become submerged, holding your breath the whole time.

Do this slowly and gradually and eventually you will become used to the feeling of breath holding and having water on your face.

Try breathing out through your mouth by blowing gently. Allow the bubbles to tickle your nose and splash your face. These feelings are all common part of swimming so practice this until you are used to it.

Feeling brave?

Step 2: Try again but this time venture a little deeper by allowing your eyes to become submerged, still holding your breath.

You might want to wear some swim goggles for this one. The ability to see everything clearly under the water can be quite calming and reassuring.

Once you are used to submerging yourself in the water, your fear of swimming is nearly conquered and you are ready to take your feet off the pool floor and begin to swim.

Fear of Swimming In Deep Water?

One important point you must understand here: the buoyancy of the human body is the same in deep water as it is in shallow water. In other words your ability to remain at the water surface is the same regardless of the depth of the water.

Try this psychological test:

Swim away from the pool side for a distance of 5 to 10 metres, but to water that is still within your standing depth. Then, change direction and swim back to the poolside you came from, but *without* touching the pool floor with your feet.

If you are able to complete this without any problems then you have just proved to yourself that you are able to stop, change direction and return to poolside in any depth of water. The fact that you managed this without putting your feet on the bottom of the pool means that the depth of the water is of no relevance whatsoever.

Real Questions

"I am 53 and just started swimming lessons a few weeks ago. I had a scary experience in the water as a child and am trying to get over my fear. I am doing fine with most exercises in the shallow end but I get terrified heading into the deep end. Any advice?"

Mark's answer:

"Swimming in the deep end can be a daunting task, especially if you have had a bad experience as a child. That experience would have left a scare in your mind that now holds you back.

Lets get a few things straight in your head first of all. Things that sound obvious but your past experience is clouding them in your head:

1. *You do not sink like a stone the moment you swim out of your depth. Your ability to float (to a certain degree) and move through the water has been proven in your lessons so far in the shallow end.*

2. *The deep water will not pull you under and does not make you float any less. Your body behaves in exactly the same way in deep water as it does in shallow water.*

Swimming in shallow water during your lessons, you have no doubt learnt how to stop and stand up mid way across the pool. You will not be able to do this in deep water (sorry to state the obvious again!), so you must now learn how to change direction as you swim or even turn around completely and swim back to the side without putting your feet on the pool floor. You can practice this in shallow water and its best in water of about chest depth.

This is key to overcoming your fear of swimming in deep water. Its about installing confidence in your own ability. If you know you can change direction as you swim and make your way to the nearest side or even back to where you swam from, then the depth of the water is completely irrelevant.

Another factor to consider is fitness and stamina. As you learn to swim your fitness and stamina will increase and improve and then so will the distances you will be able to confidently swim.

Some people make the mistake of swimming from the shallow end toward the deep end and then get themselves in difficulty as they become tired and out of breath.

If you are able to start from the pool side without your feet on the pool floor, then start from up in the deep end and swim towards the shallow end. That way as you will be nearing shallower water as you start to become out of breath will be able to put your feet down if need be.

Do you swim with googles on and with your face in the water? Swimming with googles on allows you to see clearly everything around you. Sometimes learning to swim face down can give you a greater appreciation of where you are and what you are doing. It might open your mind and you might start to enjoy and embrace the deeper water."

"I have a fear of swimming without holding my nose! I have tried swimming without holding my nose before, but I literally choked. Please don't laugh. I know it sounds so weird and stupid and hilarious, but it's true. I have tried EVERYTHING!"

Mark's answer:

"Forgive me if you think I might be stating the obvious, but you need to practice holding your breath underwater.

The reason you choke is that water is getting up your nose as you submerge your face and swim, and the only reason water goes up your nose is that you are breathing it up there.

It is most likely that you are doing this unconsciously – in other words, you are not consciously holding your breath and instead your body is attempting to breathe through your nose when you swim, without you telling it to!

Firstly take some time to practice holding your breath and submerging. Not swimming at all, but remaining in one place in the pool, feet on the floor if necessary.

If fully submerging is still causing a problem, then remain at the surface and just place your mouth and or nose in the water, and work up to fully submerging gradually.

The important thing here is to take a big enough breath in to allow you to hold it for a few seconds. So, take a large breath in, as if you're about to blow out the candles on a cake, and hold it all in.

Now this may sound like baby stuff, and you may well be more than able to do this stuff. If so, forgive me, but it is important to ensure you can do it.

17

Lets say you can easily hold your breath and submerge. The problem now is that by swimming (kicking your legs and pulling with your arms), it is causing you to exhale and inhale at the same time.

This is a question of coordination. Most people associate coordination with making your arms do something at the same time as your legs. In your case (and this is only a possible suggestion), it is the coordination of your breathing and your overall movement.

You need to teach your body to hold your breath and swim at the same time. At the point of needing to breathe again, you then need to surface to take another breath.

This goes back to remaining in one place in the pool and practicing just breathing. Submerge and move your arms and legs really slowly, keeping your breath held. Resurface and take another breath.

Keep practicing until it becomes second nature."

"I am 43 years old and I desperately want to learn how to swim, but I get very scared because I cannot touch the bottom of the pool. What can I do to overcome this?"

Mark's answer:

"The problem you are describing is actually the easiest part to deal with. The hardest part is learning to swim first of all. Learn to swim within your depth first. Learn to become comfortable in the water, learn how to stop and stand up whilst moving without your feet on the pool floor.

Once you have become happy swimming short distances within your depth, then swim a short distance in water of about shoulder depth.

Now the important part: Imagine you are not able to touch to pool floor - swim away from the side, change direction and then swim back again, all without touching your feet down and all within your depth. Practice this within your depth until you can do it confidently.

Psychologically it makes no difference what depth the water is if you are confident that you can change direction and swim to the side of the pool.

Always learn to swim gradually and at your own pace. Move on when you are confident within yourself. Rome wasn't built in a day!"

Chapter 3: Swimming Science

How Your Body Behaves In The Water

Understanding some of the key scientific principles of swimming will provide a greater understanding of how the human body behaves in water. It will also give a greater insight into how and why strokes are swum in the way that they are.

Buoyancy

It is important to understand buoyancy and relative density when learning how to swim. A basic understanding of this is a crucial element of overcoming a fear of water. Floating is a characteristic of the human body. Some of us have good buoyancy while others do not. It's all down to our relative density. In other words, how dense our body structure is, compared to the density of the water we are attempting to float in.

Let us put some actual figures to this:

- Freshwater has a density of $1g/cm^3$
- Saltwater has a density of $1.024g/cm^3$, therefore having a higher density
- The average male has a density of $0.98g/cm^3$ and the average female $0.97g/cm^3$.

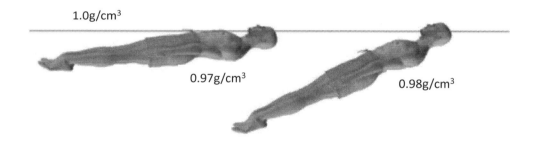

We can deduce therefore that most human beings will float to a certain degree, with a small amount of the body staying above the water surface.

Females float better than males and both males and females float better in saltwater than in freshwater. Very few adults can float horizontally in the water, yet most children can hold a star float in the horizontal position.

It must be noted that a person's weight has little to do with their density. Muscle is denser and therefore heavier than fat, making fatter people better floaters.

Other factors that effect floatation are:

- The volume of air in the lungs
- An individual's muscle to fat ratio
- The shape of the individual and therefore the position of their centre of gravity

Propulsion

Swimmers have to provide movement in the water in order to propel themselves through it. Types of movement that we use most commonly are paddling, sculling and kicking.

Paddling is likened to oars on a boat. A large flat surface area pulled in one direction causes another object to move in the opposite direction. In the case of the human body, we pull or push with our hands and arms, causing us to move backwards or forwards in the water.

Sculling takes the form of a curved shape in the water made by the hands as they move to find still, undisturbed water. Water that is not moving provides more propulsion than water that is already moving

All of the swimming strokes require some kind of sculling action. Sculling is the most efficient way of moving our hands and arms through the water.

Kicking the water with the legs is the least efficient way of moving through the water as it can require a rapid movement that can very quickly become tiring.

It can be argued that kicking, be it in an up and down motion or a curved motion as in breaststroke, is another form of paddling or sculling.

This is true, but kicking is often the first means of propulsion in the water that children discover and therefore can be classed as a separate form of propulsion.

Resistance

As the body moves through the water, it is met by resistance coming from the water itself. If this resistance is to be easily overcome, the body moving through the water has to be as streamlined as possible.

There are three main types of resistance a swimmer will encounter in the water:

• Profile resistance
• Viscous drag
• Eddy currents

Profile resistance
This is the resistance met head on by the swimmer. As the swimmer moves forward through the water, the profile resistance is pushing him back. If profile resistance is to be minimised, body shape has to be made as narrow and streamlined as possible.

Viscous drag
As a swimmer moves through the water, friction slows him down by creating a drag force. As water comes into contact with the skin, forward motion is compromised by the dragging force backwards. Excess body hair and baggy swimming shorts cause large increases in viscous drag.

Eddy currents
These are caused by an object moving through the water, causing the surrounding water to move and create turbulences. For example, if you place a floating object behind you as you swim, the object will follow you in the eddy current your swimming has created. Eddy currents are generally reduced when profile resistance is improved.

Chapter 4: Buoyancy Aids

Essential Aids for Learning To Swim

There is a wide range of swimming equipment available to help anyone learn to swim or improve their swimming strokes. It is not necessary to use all of the equipment listed here as some swimming aids will be more beneficial than others, depending on the individual.

Floatation devices and buoyancy aids are the most commonly used to help assist non swimmers, usually young children in gaining confidence in the water. Some swimming aids will be more suited to adults than to children and most equipment is not expensive to buy.

Floats or Kickboards

Swimming floats, often referred to as kickboards, are by far the most popular items of swimming equipment used by beginners learning to swim, due to their versatility and adaptability.

They are suitable for non-swimmers right up to advanced swimmers, and can be used by both adults and children.

Swim floats are used by swimming teachers as part of lessons for many different exercises. They can be used by non-swimmers to strengthen and by established swimmers to isolate and perfect technique.

For example, the weak non-swimmer can use two floats, one placed under each arm, to help strengthen their leg kick. The floats will provide stability and help boost confidence, whilst encouraging a correct and focused leg kick.

The established swimmer can hold a float in one hand whilst performing front crawl, for example, with the other arm. This allows that arm to be isolated so the swimmer can focus on that arm or maybe the breathing technique to one side.

Either way, by introducing a float into the exercise, the change in focus helps to fine-tune swimming technique.

Floats and Kickboards: Advantages and Disadvantages

Advantages:

- Very versatile and can help enhance a wide range of swimming exercises.

- Can be used in addition to other swimming aids.

- Can be used in place of other types of swimming aid to encourage progression and enhance strength and stamina.

- When used individually floats can help gain leg or arm strength.

- Fine-tune technique by encouraging a swimmer to focus on a certain area of their swimming stroke.

- Cheap to buy and easy to store.

Disadvantages:

- Not suitable for very young children or babies learning to swim.

- Require close supervision

Swim Noodle

One of the most popular buoyancy aids, the swimming noodle, is a simple polythene foam cylinder approximately 3 inches in diameter and about 58 inches long. One of the most popular and widely used floats during swimming lessons.

Sometimes called a 'woggle', it is cheap to make, cheap to buy and easy to use in large group swimming lessons.

The main advantage is that it provides a high level of support whilst as the same time allowing the swimmer movement of their arms and legs. The swimmer is able to learn and experience propulsion through the water from both the arms and the legs.

The noodle is very versatile and as it is not a fixed aid, it can be used and removed with ease. It can also add a sense of fun to swimming as it can be tucked under the arms on the front and the back as well as placed between the legs and used as a 'horse'.

Swimming Noodle: Advantages and Disadvantages

Advantages:

- Provides a high level of support for children of all sizes.

- Gives a sense of independence in the water with the minimum of support.

- Allows freedom of movement.

- Boosts confidence in the nervous beginner.

- Able to support adult beginners

- Easy to fit and remove, so ideal for using in group swimming lessons.

- Allows freedom of movement.

Disadvantages:

- Limited or no use for advanced swimmers.

- Nervous swimmers can squeeze it between their body and their arms, restricting their arm action.

- Can cause very buoyant swimmers to tip forwards.

- Tricky to pack into a suitcase, so not travel or vacation friendly.

Armbands (or Water Wings)

Armbands, sometimes known as water wings, are probably the most popular and most commonly used swimming aid for children. Armbands are very cheap and very durable floatation aids that are ideal for assisting young children in the early stages of learning to swim.

They help to keep kids afloat in the water whilst at the same time give them a sense of freedom, allowing them to kick and move about the pool independently.

Although they can be restrictive to the movement of their arms, they keep a child close to the surface of the water. This allows them to experience blowing bubbles in the water and any splashing sensations, all of which are vital parts of the learning to swim process.

Armbands: Advantages and Disadvantages

Whilst very popular, armbands are by no means perfect. They have their advantages and disadvantages.

Advantages:

- Develop early confidence - great for boosting the water confidence of young children and giving them a sense of freedom in the pool.

- Buoyancy level can be adjusted - the amount of assistance provided by armbands can be reduced by gradual deflation as the non-swimmer becomes stronger and more confident.

- Co-ordination can be enhanced and improved as a child's arms and legs can be used independently.

- A larger number of swimmers can be safely supervised, making armbands ideal for large group swimming lessons.

Disadvantages:

- Swimmers can become dependant on armbands. Some children find it difficult to change to a different swimming aid, which then holds back their progress.

- They can restrict movement. Due to the nature of how they are fitted on the arms, armbands can be restrictive and may hinder arm movement, especially in smaller children.

- May not provide enough buoyancy if used by adults. Ideally armbands are to be used only by children.

Swim Ring

A swim ring is a cheap and durable item of equipment that is ideal for the non-swimmer. It is used mainly by children as a way of enhancing their confidence the water.

The aid is worn around the body of the child and like armbands, it can restrict arm movements. It does however allow full movement and freedom of the legs.

It is vitally important to take into consideration the size of the child to be put into the ring. The child has to be large enough and strong enough to be able to support themselves within the ring.

If they are not strong enough or big enough, they will simply slip through. An alternative buoyancy aid should be considered, such as arm bands or a swim jacket.

This type of floatation device is very old fashioned but is still popular due to its low cost and durability. It's also very quick and easy to fit and remove, making it a very convenient swimming aid.

Swim Ring: Advantages and Disadvantages

Advantages:

• Allows the child's face to be kept clear of the water. They can be kept at a safe level above the water surface, reducing the risk of taking water into the mouth or nose.

• Cheap to buy and easy to deflate and store away.

• Gives complete freedom of the legs allowing the child to kick underwater.

Disadvantages:

• Can be insecure and some children can slip through. An alternative floatation aid should be used if the child is too small.

• Is usually restrictive for the arms and therefore may not allow the child to develop a sufficient arm action.

• Promotes a vertical body position. At an early age this is not an issue, but as the child grows and becomes stronger they need to develop a horizontal swimming position. An alternative swimming aid should be used, such as swim noodle.

Swim Jacket

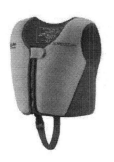

The swim jacket is a very popular and successful example of a children's swimming aid. The swim jacket, sometimes referred to as a swim vest, promotes floatation and enhances confidence in the water.

This type of child swimming jacket usually provides buoyancy at both the front and rear of the torso. This promotes an upright body position, which for a toddler learning to experience the water and move about in deep water, is perfect.

The Advantages of the Swim Jacket

One of the main advantages of this type of swimming aid is that the arms and legs are unrestricted and are free to move. This then has obvious advantages to experiencing the water and eventually learning to swim.

Most swim vests have floats contained within the lining structure of the suit and they can be removed as the child becomes more confident and stronger in the water. By removing the floats from the suit one at a time, the swim jacket's buoyancy is reduced, forcing the swimmer to work harder and therefore become stronger.

As they start to grow and become stronger, they will begin to kick their legs and move their hands and arms in the water. It is at this point a slightly more diagonal body position is needed with the legs slightly behind and the chin on the water surface.

To achieve this position whilst still wearing the vest, floats should be removed from the front of the suit so that the rear of the suit is then encouraged to float.

Back Float

Growing in popularity, the back float is a brilliant way to boost swimming ability and water confidence.

A child wearing a back float in the water will be completely buoyant and therefore completely safe. It should be noted however that all children should be supervised in the water at all times, however 'safe' a certain buoyancy aid might be.

The float is secured comfortably to the back of the swimmer using straps and clips and it works with their natural buoyancy to help achieve the correct body position gradually over time.

For example, it helps to provide support for the beginner, whose body position will be almost vertical to begin with. As the swimmer becomes more confident, the float assists and aids a more natural, horizontal position in the water.

When a complete horizontal position is achieved, the float's assistance is virtually eliminated as it is on or above the water surface.

The overall swimming experience is enhanced by the fact that arms and legs are completely free to move and explore the water. The freedom of the arms then allows the swimmer to develop strength and stamina by using a more appropriate and correct arm action technique.

For beginners learning how to swim the back float should be used in conjunction with other swimming aids. If it is used as the sole swimming aid then the swimmer can become dependant.

Back Float: Advantages and Disadvantages

Advantages:

• Works with the swimmers natural buoyancy.

• Allows completely free movement of the arms and legs.

• Can be used in conjunction with other swimming aids.

• Enhances and builds confidence by encouraging freedom of movement.

Disadvantages:

• Not suitable for babies.

• Can promote a vertical position in the water.

Pull Buoy

A pull buoy is a figure-eight shaped piece of solid foam and used mainly by established and advanced swimmers.

 It is placed between the legs in the upper thigh area to provide support to the body so the swimmer can swim without kicking the legs. This allows them to focus on other parts of their swimming stroke, such as arm or breathing technique.

This type of swimming aid is most useful when learning and practicing front crawl and backstroke swimming techniques.

These training aids are most commonly used by competitive swimmers during their training sessions. They are designed to restrict the use of the swimmer's lower body, causing a greater intensity on the arms and upper body.

The nature of holding it between the legs by squeezing the thighs together also helps to keep the lower body in a streamlined and efficient shape during the swim.

By isolating the upper body, the swimmer is able to focus completely on their arm or breathing technique, whilst the float assists to kept the lower body afloat.

They also help to strengthen the upper body and arms by eliminating the kick propulsion, while helping to keep the body position correct in the water. As the upper body is isolated during a swim using this training aid, it can cause the core muscles to have to work, resulting in increased core strength.

Pull Buoy: Advantages and Disadvantages

Advantages:

- Provides good isolation of the upper body whilst keeping the lower body buoyant.

- Ideal for work-outs and training and therefore best suited to established and advanced swimmers.

- Increased core strength.

- Available in adult and junior sizes.

Disadvantages:

- Not suitable for non-swimmers and beginners.

Chapter 5: Entering The Pool

Safe Entries Into The Pool

Entering the swimming pool can be either hugely daunting or very exciting for the non swimmer. Either way, it must be done in a safe and appropriate way.

Before entering any swimming pool it is important to establish which end of the pool is the deep end and which is the shallow end. Most pools have appropriate signs up that clearly show which end is which. Most will also state the depth of the water at each end.

If you are unable to establish the water depth at your chosen point of entry, then ask the lifeguard on duty. Some swimming pools have no deep or shallow end, but instead are the same depth throughout.

The Most Common Safe Entries Into Water

Those new to swimming and learning how to swim should consider the following methods of entering the pool:

- using the poolside steps
- the sitting swivel entry
- jumping entry

Stepping in Using the Poolside Steps

This is the best entry for the nervous non-swimmer. Check the depth of the water first to ensure you can stand on the pool floor once you have fully entered the water. Enter by holding on to the rails with both hands and stepping down one step at a time.

This is a safe and gradual entry that allows you to take your time.

Some pools have steps into the pool underwater that start at deck level. These are the safest and easiest entry points as they allow a slow and gradual entry.

The Sitting Swivel Entry

This entry works best on deck-level swimming pools. Once again ensure the water depth is shallow enough to be able to stand on the pool floor before entering.

From a sitting position, with legs in the water, place both hands to one side and then turn your back to the water. Lower yourself gradually into the water, keeping hold of the poolside at all times.

Jumping Entry

A jumping entry into the swimming pool is usually appropriate for the confident swimmer. Non swimmers and those with a fear of swimming in deep water are unlikely to be confident enough to jump into the water unaided.

Confident non-swimmers might jump into the pool, but should do so wearing appropriate buoyancy aids.

Before using a jumping entry, the swimmer should consider the depth of the water compared to their own height.

Start with toes over the edge of the poolside, jump away from the poolside and bend the knees on landing.

Real Questions

"I lack everything about swimming. I want to learn some basic swimming tips and exactly what to do to keep afloat. What do I do with the arms and the legs? I tried on my own but the basic techniques are lacking. I just do not know what to do when I enter the water. Everyone, including the kids will notice immediately that I am not a swimmer. Please help me."

Mark's answer:

"First of all it does not matter who will notice that you are not a swimmer. There are many adults who cannot swim and wish they could, but most of those stay away from the pool because they are embarrassed.

You have had the courage to enter the swimming pool and have a go, which is a major step for most adult beginners.

The fact that you have tried on your own tells me that you have no fear of water, so learning to swim should be an easy process.

The easiest swimming stroke to learn as an adult is breaststroke because it is the least tiring and most comfortable to try out. The arms pull in a circular motion and the legs kick in a powerful whip like circle to provide the propulsion to move through the water.

The timing of the arms and legs for breaststroke can sometimes be tricky, but as long as you pull THEN kick, it should come together.

Essential swimming basics that you must learn are how to hold your breath, submerge your face and breathe out under the water. Practicing this will help you to become more relaxed in the water.

Once you become more relaxed you will find it easier to remain afloat, although floating is not something that we are all able to do. Some of us naturally sink, especially our legs, but a good combination of swimming technique and relaxing into our swimming helps us stay at the water surface.

Learning how to stop and stand up mid swim is also an important basic to learn so that you can stop if you get tired and stand up, providing you are within your own depth."

"I am experiencing fear when learning to dive. How I can reduce my fear when I dive?"

Mark's answer:

"The fear associated with diving usually comes from the fact that you are attempting to enter the water head first from a physically higher position. Therefore the water seems further away and diving in head first is a completely unnatural thing to do.

First and most importantly of all ensure that the water you will be diving into is safe to do so. Is it clear and can you see the pool floor? Is it deep enough or is the water shallow? Diving into water that is not deep enough is extremely dangerous.

The ideal diving depth is your own height with your arms extended above your head.

A shallow dive (a dive across the surface of the water) is safe in most cases but only after it has been practiced and with adequate supervision and guidance.

To remove your fear, start with a sitting dive. Sit on the edge of the pool with your feet back against the wall. The safest diving position is with your arms stretched out in front and head tucked in between them for protection. Aim for your finger tips to enter the water first, followed by your head, with it tucked safely between your arms.

Starting with a sitting dive will remove the fear of diving from a height and get you used to entering the water head first.

You can then progress to a kneeling dive, diving from kneeling on one knee. This is a little higher and will help build your confidence to dive from standing up.

When diving from standing up, bend your knees and start very low down, almost as low as your sitting or kneeling dives. Then as your confidence grows your diving will become fearless!"

Chapter 6: Learning To Go Underwater

Submerging and Going Underwater

Submerging and going underwater for the beginner is a skill that is best achieved in a step-by-step process. Breath holding exercises and basic submerging exercises are a good starting point for non-swimmers.

Being relaxed is the key here and relaxation in the water is discussed in more detail in a later chapter. The more relaxed you are in the water, the less oxygen is used by our body and then the length of time spent underwater increases.

The ability to submerge the face is arguably one of the most important stages when learning to swim, particularly when overcoming a fear of water.

Some beginners arrive with this ability built in and only need to be taught how to breathe whilst swimming. For others it can be one of the most terrifying tasks they face.

Three Basic Stages To Swimming Underwater

There are three key steps to work through to become confident with submerging underwater. These are crucial for beginners and for those with a fear of water. Others will find them easy. The 3 steps are:

1. Getting the face wet.

2. Taking a breath and partially submerging.

3. Total submersion and swim underwater.

It goes without saying that a gradual approach is needed here. One stage at a time and only when you are happy and confident do you proceed to the next stage.

Stage 1: Getting the face wet

Remember, getting the face wet and being splashed in the face are two completely different concepts, each having different effects, and not always positive ones. Here are a few practices to work through:

Blowing bubbles on the water surface or blowing an object along as you swim or walk through the water. You can either blow gently "like blowing through a straw" or blow with force "like blowing out candles on a cake".

Cupping water in your own hands and throwing it onto your face is also a sure way of getting used to having a wet face.

Throwing and catching a ball is an excellent distraction from the splashes of the water. If the ball is made to land just in front of you, this will result in a wet face without too much concern due to the distraction of catching the ball. The smallest of splashes from the softest of throws will be sufficient to have a positive effect.

Stage 2: Partially submerging the face

The next stage of mastering going underwater is to learn how to hold your breath by "breathing in and holding it all in".

 Some will be able to do this easily, others will learn by trial and error as you partially submerge your face and realise you are not able to breath underwater!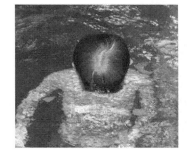

An object can then be placed just under the water surface, shallow enough to see and reach for it, but deep enough for the mouth to be submerged in order to reach it.

Once confidence is gained with this exercise, then the object can be lowered slightly to encourage the mouth and nose to be submerged.

These practices are best performed with an assistant in the water holding the object for you. This may also help enhance your confidence with someone in the water beside you.

Stage 3: Total Submersion

Stage 2 naturally leads quickly onto stage 3 where the object is placed below the water surface where you are encouraged to retrieve it by completely submerging your head underwater.

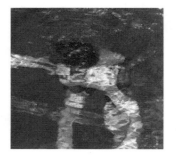

By this stage, breath holding should be more accomplished and you should begin to relax more as you submerge.

Progression from this stage is to incorporate face submerging, either partially or completely, whilst swimming various strokes and even retrieving objects from the pool floor as you swim.

All of the above stages assist hugely with the overall process of learning how to swim.

Understanding your own buoyancy is important as this can be a crucial factor that can dictate how easy going underwater will be. If your body has good buoyancy, then submerging and swimming underwater is more difficult, although not impossible.

Real Questions

"My question is about going underwater without holding your nose. This is something I've never been able to do. Water always goes up my nose and into my sinuses. I've tried blowing out of my nose when I first go under, slow submersion and no matter what I still wind up with water creeping down the back of my throat. Am I doing something wrong?"

Mark's answer:

"Your problem is all too common in adults. I see it all the time - adults going underwater and having to hold their noses. I don't blame you for not wanting to wear a nose clip!

Please forgive me for asking what is probably an obvious question, but are you actually holding your breath? Are you taking a deep breath and then stopping yourself from breathing whilst you submerge?

The reason I ask it that the only way water can enter your nose and sinuses, when you are upright in the pool, is if you breathe it up there. It is possible to think you are holding your breath when you are actually still breathing.

Before you strike me down for asking stupid questions, consider this:

Your nose and sinuses contain air. The only way in and out of your body for that air is through your mouth or nose. Assuming your mouth is closed, as you submerge the water causes an airlock in your nose. In other words, the water is stopping the air from getting out and the air is stopping the water from getting in.

Imagine an empty bottle turned upside down and then submerged. The air in the bottle has nowhere to go and it is preventing the water from entering it. The only way water enters the bottle is when the bottle is returned the right way up with the opening at the top. Water forces the air out and fills the bottle.

Swimmers experience water in their nose when they try to perform forward somersaults or flip turns because they are momentarily turned upside down, allowing air to escape and water to get it.

In your case, you could be unconsciously breathing in as your nose gets wet. Yes, your nostrils and just inside your nose will get wet, but not enough to completely flood your sinuses and back of your throat. Sometimes that feeling and sensation of getting water on the face can trigger a breathing response. It is quite common.

I guess the only way to find out is to practice holding your breath. Have contests with your kids to see who can hold their breath the longest - not in the pool, just generally anywhere. Then take your contest to the pool and try it there. Take a deep breath and then submerge just your mouth and nose, nothing else. Keep your eyes out. You remain in an upright position with air an airlock in your nose (remember the empty bottle), and no water should enter your nose at all."

"Being your best is not so much about overcoming the barriers other people place in front of you as it is about overcoming the barriers we place in front of ourselves."

Kieren Perkins - Four-time Olympic Swimming Medalist

Chapter 7: Standing Up Mid Swim

How To Stand Up Mid Swim

Stopping and standing up from swimming is an often overlooked part of learning to swim. Once you are able to stop yourself and place your feet back down on the pool floor, your confidence will take a massive boost.

Whatever your standard of swimming, knowing that as long as you are within your depth, you can stop and stand up when you become tired or anxious, you confidence will in turn be enhanced.

Complete beginners can start from holding the poolside and practice bending their knees forward and placing their feet on the pool floor. They can then progress to holding floats under each arm and performing the same movement.

As confidence grows, the swimmer can attempt standing without assistance, which requires a greater use of the arms and hands. This can also be progressed to a moving exercise, moving first towards and then away from the poolside.

Standing Up From A Prone (Face Down) Position

Movement should be relaxed and smooth, knees are drawn forward as the arms simultaneously pull downward and backwards as the head lifts and faces forward.

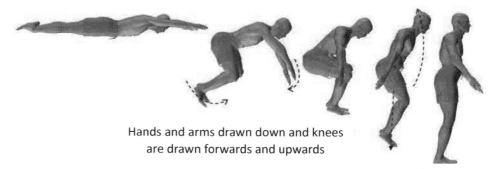

Hands and arms drawn down and knees
are drawn forwards and upwards

Hands pull backwards as the
head lifts and the feet are
placed on the pool floor

Key Focus Points

- Pull down and back with both arms.
- Bend your knees forwards as if to sit.
- Lift your head upwards.
- Place your feet on the pool floor.

46

Common Faults

- The movement is rushed and not relaxed.
- Failure to bend the knees.
- Arching the back.
- Failure to pull down and back with the hands

Standing Up From A Supine (Face Up) Position

The movement should be relaxed and smooth as the knees are drawn towards the chest. The arms pull upwards and forwards and the head should lift and face forward as the feet are placed on the pool floor.

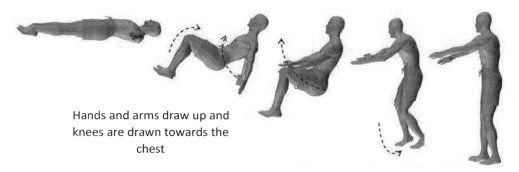

Hands and arms draw up and knees are drawn towards the chest

Hands pull upwards as the head lifts and the feet are placed on the pool floor

Key Points

- Pull both arms upwards to the surface.
- Bend your knees forwards as if to sit.
- Lift your head upwards.
- Place your feet on the pool floor.

Common Faults

- Movement is rushed and not relaxed.
- Failure to bend the knees.
- Arching the back.
- Failure to pull up with both arms

Real Questions

"Last year it was my New Year's resolution to learn to swim, I did have a fear of water and gained a bit of confidence when I went to aqua aerobics. I'm just worried that when I do learn with floats I won't be able to get my feet off the floor. Please help!"

Mark's answer:

"Well done for getting in the water and having a go at aqua aerobics. That is no mean feat when you have a fear of water. Aqua aerobics is great for getting used to the water and discovering a bit about how your body moves and behaves in the water. However it doesn't teach you about floating, holding your breath and all the important stuff when it comes to learning how to swim.

As for getting your feet off the floor, believe it or not, that is not the scary part. The scary part is working out how to get them back down and safely onto the pool floor again. Once you can do this, you will feel a little more confident about lifting your feet up and trying some swimming.

Like most adult beginners you will most probably be wondering about floating and how you float. This is all down to your body shape and composition. You will find that either you float easily or you do not float at all. Some people are good floaters and some are not so. But, even the bad floaters can learn to swim.

If you are a poor floater, keep in mind that the human body does not sink like a stone. You will sink very slowly and gently, which allows for some time to add arm pulls and leg kicks to help keep your body at or near the water surface.

Your first exercise to try out is holding the pool side, or better still a trusty friends hands, and lift your feet up off the floor. Then try bending your knees forwards under your body and placing your feet back down on the floor again. You can do this with the security of holding something or someone and this will help massively with regaining a standing position again.

You can then progress, when you're ready, to holding the poolside, and then letting go just as you stand up. You will have to use your arms and hands to pull down through the water to help to stand again. Doing it near the pool side will give you the added security of grabbing it if you need to.

An absolute must for you to learn is holding your breath and putting your face in the water. Use some goggles as this makes it a little easier. Once again practice this whilst holding the poolside, breathing out into the water, lifting your face out taking another breath and then repeating the exercise. The more you do this the more it will become second nature and your fears will gradually disappear."

"Learning to stand up is holding me back. I have had 12 months of one-to-one lessons with a fantastic teacher - teaching me to float, glide (inc torpedo glide)breaststroke arms and kicks, on my back...going great but I need to (lightly) touch her with my fingertips to stand back up. I have an irritating switch in my head that tells me I can't do it on my own, yet we both know I can. How do I get past this?"

Mark's answer:

"From what you have told me, as a beginner you have conquered several major hurdles – hurdles that are the cause of many psychological barriers, the main ones being floating and gliding. I presume you are able to perform these with your face submerged? If not then this is the source of your problem. Holding your breath and submerging unaided (even in water of standing depth) conquers many psychological barriers.

I shall assume you are fine with holding your breath and floating and gliding face down.

The technique of standing up is a simultaneous combination of pulling down through the water with both arms whilst bending the knees forward into an almost sitting position, before placing the feet on the pool floor. I'm guessing you have pretty much got this movement well practiced – just not completely on your own yet!

The most common mistake made when attempting to stand is to lift the head first, resulting in an arching of the back causing the legs to remain at or near the water surface. Followed usually by some form of panic.

The first movement should be both arms pulling deep down in the water followed instantly by drawing the knees up underneath. Only then do you think about lifting the head.

Try floating or gliding towards the poolside, lightly touch the poolside and then stand up, but without bearing your weight or using the poolside in anyway. The light touch should be for your own psychological security. Once this becomes easy then try it without touching the poolside at all. Psychologically the poolside is there for you should you need it but hopefully you won't.

This exercise will also help you stand without your teacher being present in the pool (which could be hindering you without you realising it).

Standing up should be a slow gradual and relaxed movement, not a sudden fast movement. Keep your face in the water for a little longer whilst you move your arms and legs and take your time over the whole movement.

If you end up pulling down with one arm and standing on one leg whilst falling slightly sideways, then so what – you stood up. You get no extra points for technical merit here!

Look at it from another point of view. Most adults can hold their breath for at least 10 seconds and it takes 2 or 3 seconds to slowly stand from a prone position. So what's the worst that's going to happen? You have your face in the water for a couple of seconds more than you first intended and your teacher gives you a little helping hand.

As an experiment see how long you can hold you breath for. Lets say you can do it for 15 seconds. Then make a deal with your swimming teacher that you will float for a maximum of 15 seconds (or whatever time you are comfortable holding your breath for). In that time you will attempt to stand up without assistance and only after 15 seconds will you teacher offer their hands as support. At least then you are trying to stand unaided.

The key points to remember are to relax, perform the movement slowly and place your feet on the pool floor before lifting you head up."

Chapter 8: How To Float

Why We Sink and How To Float

How do I float? Probably the most common question asked by beginners learning to swim. Adults especially are curious as to why some people can float and why some people sink?

Let us dispel some myths first of all...

Myth #1 - The harder and faster I kick, the more I will stay afloat.
Not true. Harder kicking almost always results in sinking.

Myth #2 - The faster I use my arms the more I will stay afloat.
Not true either. A faster arm action will not assist the body to stay up any more than a slower one.

Myth #3 - The water is trying to pull me down.
The water is in fact trying to support you.

Myth #4 - If I take a bigger breath and hold it for longer I will float.
A bigger inhalation of air is not enough to prevent your legs from sinking.

The Psychology Of Floating: What's going on in your head?

It is common in beginners and those with a fear of water to think that the water is pulling them down. As an adult learning to swim it is important to understand that the water is actually trying to support you.

The human body does not sink like a stone. Those of us that naturally sink, usually sink slowly and gradually.

So with that in mind, we have to move our arms and legs in a way that help the water to support us. Those movements can be very subtle, small ones or they may have to be larger movements to help generate some momentum.

Either way, most of us have to do our bit to help the water to support us. It is a matter of discovering our own level of buoyancy, which may not necessarily be at the water surface.

Why Do We Sink?

Floating is a characteristic of the human body. Some of us have good buoyancy while others do not. It is all down to our relative density. In other words, how dense our body structure is, compared to the density of the water we are attempting to float in.

Let us be reminded of the figures from the Swimming Science chapter:

- Freshwater has a density of $1g/cm^3$
- Saltwater has a higher density of $1.024g/cm^3$

The average male has a density of $0.98g/cm^3$ and the average female $0.97g/cm^3$. We can deduce therefore that most human beings will float to a certain degree, with a small amount of the body staying above the water surface.

The diagram below shows our relative density compared to freshwater, which has a relative density of 1 gram per cubic centimetre ($1g/cm^3$).

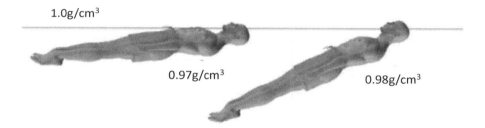

$1.0g/cm^3$

$0.97g/cm^3$

$0.98g/cm^3$

Generally speaking people that are muscular, lean or thin will tend to sink. Those that have a wider surface area or a larger body fat percentage will usually remain afloat for longer. That said, everybody's legs tend to sink eventually.

Do You Naturally Sink?

The simple facts are that fat floats and muscle sinks. Yes, fat people are better floaters than thin, or muscular people.

Generally speaking our legs are heavy and therefore sink and our upper body will tend to float because our lungs contain air. But, the higher our body fat percentage the better chance we have of naturally staying afloat.

However, a person with low body fat percentage who is lean and has a higher density, can remain at the water surface as they swim. This is despite the fact their body naturally wants to sink.

Relax and Glide, Then Floating Becomes Easier

Feel your way through the water, don't fight your way through it. Learning how to relax in the pool will erase tension as you learn how your body moves and behaves in water.

A gliding action through the water as you swim is key to relaxing and the momentum of a glide helps to remain at the water surface and prevent sinking.

Moving through the water smoothly and with minimum effort is essential for the natural sinker to stay afloat.

Relaxing and gliding are covered in more detail in their own chapters.

Floating Stationary vs Floating As You Swim

Yes, there is a big difference. If you are not a natural floater, generally a lean or muscular person, then you will most likely sink as you remain stationary in the water. Our legs are heavy, and usually sink first. A poor floater can however remain at or near the water surface as they swim, providing they are relaxed and have some degree of swimming technique.

The propulsion gained from arm pulls and leg kicks generates momentum, which in turn aids in keeping a swimmer afloat as they move through the water.

Which Swimming Stroke Is Best For Staying Afloat?

Beginners learning to swim breaststroke will find floating easier than those learning to swim front crawl.

This is because the arm and leg movements of breaststroke are wider and therefore cover a larger surface area of water, making it easier to remain there.

The body position for breaststroke is angled so that the leg kick can occur slightly deeper under the water, favouring those of us that tend to sink.

54

A powerful leg kick and correct timing and coordination are essential to preventing a breaststroke swimmer from sinking.

Front crawl is a more streamlined stroke and therefore has a longer and more narrow shape. This makes it more difficult, especially for the legs, to stay up near the surface as they kick.

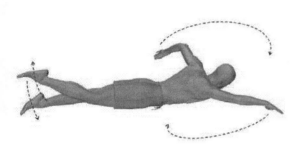

A relaxed and flowing front crawl leg kick is essential to keep the legs up near the surface. A faster, harder and more forceful kick will almost certainly result in the legs sinking quicker.

Front crawl relies on its arm action to generate most of its propulsion and movement.

Real Questions

"Why do my legs sink when swimming? I am a 75-year old male who has gone back to swimming after 60 years because arthritis doesn't allow me to do much else. I am doing ok, but it seems I have to kick excessively hard to keep my body level. Could it be that my legs are unusually dense? Is it something about my physique or am I doing something very wrong?"

Mark's answer:

"Your problem could be related to a combination of technique and your relative density. First and foremost, you must relax when you swim. The golden rule is to feel your way through the water, not fight through it. More often than not, the harder you try, the more you are likely to sink.

Not everyone is naturally buoyant in the water and in fact most males sink. This does not mean you will never be able to swim properly. You just have to adjust your technique accordingly.

The leg kick for freestyle is required to provide balance to the whole stroke and is not required for propulsion, especially over longer distances. Freestyle arms provide the power and drive for the overall stroke.

Pointing your toes and kicking with a relaxed ankle is essential, firstly to keep the legs streamlined, but also the relaxed ankle gives a fin-like kick. You could maybe try some fins as they will force your toes to point and give you a feel for kicking in a slower more relaxed way. Do not become dependent on them though!"

"I am 32, just had my first class and seem to panic when floating. I am able to float but after a few seconds I panic and try to get up abruptly. This is affecting my glide as well. I don't think I am scared, but I can't seem to control this impulse to get out, and quickly. Help please!"

Mark's answer:

"Do not stress at this stage about floating and gliding. The panic you are experiencing is very common. It can be caused by a combination of things.

If you hold your breath whilst floating or gliding, in fact if you hold your breath whilst doing anything (not even swimming related), it causes a build up of carbon dioxide in your lungs which after a few seconds needs to be released to allow in fresh oxygen. In other words you need to breathe!

Instead try to breathe out slowly as you float or glide. This will allow the carbon dioxide to be released slowly whilst you are face down in the water, which in turn will help you to relax and then make the need to breath again much less urgent.

Another factor to consider is your own buoyancy. You say you are able to float but there will almost certainly be parts of your body that will slowly sink (probably your legs) and when you glide you may find yourself beginning to roll slightly, or certainly feel unbalanced in some way. This is just the way that the human body behaves in the water and it is these kinds of things that cause the panic to quickly set in.

With all this in mind, think about your scenario. You are learning a brand new skill in an environment that quite frankly human beings were not designed to be in and do not belong in. You take in a deep breath, put your face down in the water and glide or float. Carbon dioxide builds up and you suddenly need to breathe. Combine that with an unbalanced feeling and maybe slight sinking feeling and thats it - panic. Get me out of here!

Take each lesson one at a time. Over time you will learn how your body behaves in the water when you are floating, gliding and swimming. Remember the water is not trying to pull you down. It is actually trying to support you and in time you will learn to relax and appreciate and feel your own buoyancy."

Chapter 9: How To Relax In The Water

Relax And Be At One With The Water

Being 'at one' with the water helps to ensure that everything you do in the water and when you swim is second nature and not stressful. Learning how to relax in the water and relax when swimming are vital components for the beginner master.

Essential elements of learning how to relax in the water are:

• Learning how to breath hold and submerge
• Learn how to move through the water slowly
• Learn how to breathe regularly

Go Underwater and Really Experience It

Submerging completely under the water is a great way to learn how to relax. Grab a pair of swim goggles, put them on your eyes, take a deep breath and down you go.

What do you see? Everything very clearly, so you have a very clear perception of where you are and what you are doing.

What can you hear? Not much, if anything. All is peaceful and quiet.

Now try slowly moving about. Notice how gracefully you can move, almost like moving around on the moon without gravity. That is the water trying to support and lift you.

Obviously you can only do this for as long as you can hold your breath, but the more you do it, the more you get a feel for how your body behaves in the water.

As you get more of a feel for the water you will start to get an idea of your level of buoyancy. This means you can gradually work out how much or how little movement is required from your arms and legs to keep you at or near the water surface.

You don't actually have to do any swimming when you do this. Just go underwater and experiment. Play around. Get a feel for the water and eventually you become more comfortable and relaxed.

Slower Is Better

There is a common misconception in beginners learning how to swim, that the harder we kick, pull or paddle then the better our chances are of remaining at the water surface and actually swimming some distance. This is not true.

Quite often the harder we kick, pull or paddle the less we move through the water and eventually we begin to sink.

The first rule of relaxing when we swim is to move slowly. Now you are thinking 'but if I move slowly I will sink'..? That is partly true, but if you move slowly you get a feel for the water and then begin to relax when swimming.

You must learn to 'feel' your way through the water and not 'fight' your way through it. Get the concept into your head that the water is trying to support and hold you up.

Beginners learning how to swim often think that the water is something that is trying to pull them down and that they have to fight to stay on top. This is particularly common in people that may have a fear of water or fear of swimming.

Water does not behave like that. Even those of us who do not float naturally and tend to sink, we sink very slowly and gradually. By moving our arms and legs in some kind of swimming manner, we are simply doing our bit to help the water to support us.

Breathe Before You Need To

Breathing regularly when we swim helps to keep us relaxed and calm.

It is very common to either hold our breath or exhale in the water to the point of exhaustion. The result being a frantic and panic stricken gasp for breath before submerging the face and repeating the pattern again.

So, breathe long before you need to. Don't wait for your breath to completely run out. Take a new breath at a point that is comfortable and easy to do so. You wouldn't breathe out to the point of exhaustion when running or cycling, so why do it when you swim?

Now you have become used to submerging underwater, you can move around with slow, gentle movements and you can breathe at comfortable moments when you need to. Everything you do in the water is now more relaxed. Your body is more relaxed.

Now apply these concepts and practices to your swimming technique and swim with a relaxed smooth stroke.

Real Questions

"I have tried to learn to swim a few times but I sink like a rock. I want to succeed this time so any help would be greatly appreciated."

Mark's answer:

"Your determination to succeed is to be admired. Learning to swim will open up many very pleasurable avenues in life as well as many health benefits.

Thinking that you sink like a rock is very common, even in beginners that can actually float. The trick is to relax, which I'm sure you have been told to do a few times before now, but relaxing in the water is easier said than done.

If you are even slightly anxious or nervous about swimming then your muscles will tense and your movements will be awkward and almost robotic.

So how do we learn to relax? Quite easily once you have practiced some basic stages.

The water is a completely unnatural environment for us human beings to be in and the most unnatural part is being under the water. We cannot breathe, we are not fish!

If we can understand and learn how our body behaves in the water and how to become comfortable with being submerged then swimming along at the surface will be a whole lot easier.

First thing to learn is how to hold your breath and submerge. Do this standing in water of about shoulder depth and hold your breath for about 5 seconds if you can. If you are not comfortable with this at all then start with holding your breath and lowering your mouth and nose into the water but keep your eyes out.

Once you become comfortable with this try submerging a little further. Maybe wear some swim goggles so that you can see clearly under the water. Being able to see everything clearly under the water sometimes helps a huge amount.

Next stage is to hold your breath, submerge and then allow your feet to come up from the pool floor. The air in your lungs will assist your floatation and if you lay forward slightly you may find your feet come up from the floor.

You may want to do this near to the poolside or even holding the poolside so that you are able to easily stand up again.

Once you have become comfortable with all of this then try it away from the poolside and learn to stand up for yourself.

Notice so far we have done no swimming as such. All we are doing is learning to relax so that we can help our body remain at or near the water surface when we do actually swim. Learn to submerge, lift your feet off the pool floor and then regain your standing position again. The more you practice this the more relaxed you will become in the water.

When it comes to adding some arm pulls and leg kicks, for whatever swimming stroke you wish to learn, a combination of your relaxation and your movement through the water will prevent you from sinking.

There is one very important aspect to swimming that is very often misunderstood and it is key to relaxing and swimming with ease. Do not fight your way through the water. You must feel you way through it.

If you try to swim slowly you will find you can swim just as far using half the energy than if you thrash around trying to swim fast. Relax and take your time and your success will come."

"The water is your friend...you don't have to fight with water, just share the same spirit as the water, and it will help you move."

Alexandr Popov - Olympic Gold Medallist

Chapter 10: How To Glide Through The Water

Gliding: The Missing Link To Relaxing And Floating

Gliding in aquatic terms is the concept of floating through the water, either at the surface or underwater, without assistance or movement from the arms or legs. It usually begins with a forceful push from the poolside or solid edge in order to generate some propulsion.

A streamlined body shape is important for a glide to gain and maintain some distance.

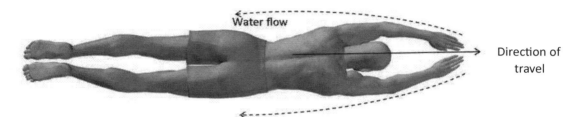

Streamlined body position minimises drag, allowing efficient movement through the water

Your personal body shape is not relevant here. We are not talking about how short, tall, fat or thin you are. Any body shape can glide through the water. It is a matter of what position you have your arms and legs in as you glide.

Your hands and feet must be together to give a pointed streamlined shape so that the water moves easily around you as your body cuts through it. If your hands and feet are apart your body shape will be creating resistance and your movement will be little, if any.

The First Few Glides Can Be Scary

The thought of gliding through the water can be a scary one for a beginner learning to swim. That wobbly and unbalanced feeling as you move through the water unaided and without using your arms and legs, can be a very strange one.

Therefore it is important to start slowly. As you get used to the feeling of gliding you can push away harder and glide further. The more you repeat this, the more you will get used to how your body behaves in the water. This will then help to relax your body and mind.

Those of us that are not natural floaters will begin to discover the point at which we sink, as our glide begins to slow. We can also learn how fast we sink, which in reality is actually very slow no matter how heavy we are.

As our glide slows and we begin to sink, we can apply some basic movements to help maintain the glide and prevent us sinking.

Combine your relaxed glide through the water with some gentle but effective arm and leg movements and you will soon discover that you float and remain at the surface as you swim.

Real Questions

"I would like to know how to glide further without sinking? I can only glide a very short distance, maybe 2-3 body lengths before I start sinking. I am a sinker so this may be a part of it, but I know I can do better. I hold my arms tight to my head to try and streamline when I push off the wall. Any suggestions for how I might be able to go further?"

Mark's answer:

"If you have already established that you are a 'sinker', my question to you would be, how do you know you can do better?

Assuming your hands and feet are together as you push away from the wall to maximise your streamlining, then it sounds to me like you are doing everything you need.

I am a sinker myself and can glide maybe 3 body lengths before I begin to slow down and sink.

The momentum you gain from your push off and your overall body shape in the water determine the rate that you slow down. Your relative density then determines the rate at which you sink.

The only other factor that will influence the distance you travel is the resistance of the water against your body. Reducing or removing body hair, wearing a tight fitting swimming costume and wearing a swim hat will all help to reduce your resistance to the water, if you want to go to these extremes.

The other factors are harder to influence. Your body shape is your body shape and maximising its streamlined efficiency (hands and feet together, head tucked down, body position flat) is probably as much as you can do.

Your relative density is difficult to change in a short time and becoming fitter and stronger will only make your muscles more dense and therefore heavier, which is really not a bad thing! People with more body fat tend to float better but decreasing body fat is preferable, so lets not go there!

The real art of swimming comes from taking your most efficient streamlined body shape and maintaining it throughout whichever stroke you swim.

Experimenting with your body shape by pushing off the wall is a great exercise to practice but it is only the beginning. Keeping your streamlined body shape throughout your swimming strokes is an entirely different challenge."

Chapter 11: How And When To Breathe

Breathing: When, How and How Often?

What is wrong with my breathing technique? Probably the most commonly question a swimming teacher gets asked.

There are a few points to consider and tips to try out in the pool to help make your breathing easier as you swim...

It all comes down to how to breathe, when to breathe and how often to breathe. All of which will depend on which stroke you are swimming.

The breathing technique for front crawl is slightly different to the breathing technique for breaststroke. However there are some similarities and common mistakes.

The 2 most common swimming breathing mistakes

When it comes to breathing during swimming, whichever swimming stroke you are attempting to swim, there are two common mistakes that many adults make:

- Holding the breath
- Breathing too late

Do Not Hold Your Breath!

We hold our breath, even though we think we are breathing out into the water. Our breath is held instinctively without knowing it. Therefore when it comes to taking a breath we have to breathe out and in again in the short split second our mouth is out of the water. This is too short a time to breathe in a controlled way and usually results in a mouth full of water.

Also, holding our breath causes a rapid increase in carbon dioxide in our respiratory system. This in turn increases the urgency to breathe again because carbon dioxide is a waste product that needs to be exhaled. The net result is more frequent and rapid breaths.

Not good when you're trying to relax and swim.

The solution is to ensure you are breathing out into the water as you swim. Breathe out in a slow controlled way without forcing the air out so that when you turn your head to breathe in again, inhaling is all you need to do and you have plenty of time to do it comfortably.

Breathe Before You Need To

The second most common mistake it to leave it right to the last second to take a breath. In other words we wait until all oxygen has completely expired and we are almost gasping for air. We turn our head to breathe and the action becomes a rushed panic that can sometimes result in a mouth full of water.

The solution here is to breath long before you need to.

Breathe IN

Breathe OUT

Breathing technique for front crawl

Set yourself a certain number of arm pulls (3 or 4 is usually most comfortable for front crawl) and breathe at that set point. The breathing pattern will change as you become more tired over time, but at least breathing in general should be easier.

Combine breathing out into the water in a slow, controlled way with taking breaths early.

Providing your swimming overall is relaxed and smooth and you have decent technique, you should find yourself swimming longer distances and becoming less exhausted.

That is the theory of easier swimming breathing and it will of course take practice and time.

What actually happens when you hold your breath?

Breath holding is an unnatural act for a human being to carry out. That is why some people find it difficult and even stressful.

The human body has several responses to breath holding and some additional responses to being submerged in water. It is how we deal with these responses that determine how comfortable or uncomfortable we are and in turn, what duration of time we are able to spend underwater whilst holding our breath.

Firstly, the amount of air we are able to inhale into our lungs depends on the size of our lungs. It may seem obvious but a taller person will have larger lungs, and therefore will be able fill them with more oxygen and can generally remain underwater for longer.

Breathe IN

Breathe OUT

Breathing technique for breaststroke

Whilst we are holding our breath, the amount of oxygen in our lungs decreases as it is carried away in the blood stream and used by the vital organs in our body. Carbon dioxide is in turn collected and returned back to the lungs. Carbon dioxide is a waste product and when a certain level is reached a signal is sent to the brain to tell us to breath again. The carbon dioxide is exhaled, fresh oxygen is inhaled and the process starts again.

Changes in heart rate occur whilst breath holding and the more relaxed we are, the slower we consume oxygen and therefore the longer we can remain holding our breath.

Submerging under the water brings about its own stresses, especially for a beginner learning swimming breathing. The experience can be made easier by wearing goggles or a mask so that the eyes can remain open, giving the person an awareness of their surroundings and therefore helping to keep them in a relaxed state.

Relaxing is the key to swimming breathing

Relaxation underwater is governed mainly by a slow heart rate. As heart rate increases so does oxygen consumption and therefore levels of stress and anxiety.

Movement of any part of the body will increase heart rate and with it oxygen consumption.

Holding our breath underwater is made easier by slowly breathing out short bursts of air. This expels carbon dioxide, reducing the amount present in the lungs. This then delays the trigger to breath.

Real Questions

"I'm learning to swim late in life, having been virtually phobic about the idea for years, and I'm having difficulty in learning to breathe in breaststroke. I've learnt to swim the strokes underwater and now I have to come up to breathe and I'm finding it really hard. I can get the head-raise fine, and I open my mouth, but just can't seem to breathe in without getting a lung-full of water, or not really breathing in at all, and just opening my mouth. Any advice would be really welcome."

Mark's answer:

"Congratulations on overcoming your near phobia, taking the plunge and learning to swim.

Breaststroke breathing technique is enormously frustrating for an adult to learn because in theory it's a simple action and yet physically it's tricky to get the hang of, especially for an adult.

Take a few steps back for a moment, so we can put things into some perspective. Adults notoriously take a long time to learn how to swim, regardless of their past experiences, phobias and abilities. There are several factors that contribute to this, the most relevant being:

- *Ability (or inability) to relax*
- *Flexibility (or lack of)*
- *Relative density (how well you float, or sink as the case may be)*

Combine these with your own perception of what you are supposed to do when you swim, and the result is a very awkward, almost robotic swimming stroke that goes nowhere fast. This usually occurs regardless of how well you think you're doing.

Don't get me wrong. What you have achieved so far is monumental. It's getting over that final hurdle that is the most frustrating.

Take the above factors and apply them to your breaststroke breathing technique.

71

For breaststroke breathing to occur smoothly and seamlessly, the stroke has to have:

- *A powerful whip kick to help give the body some lift*
- *A slightly downwards arm pull to assist the body lift*
- *Exhalation to take place underwater to allow inhalation above the water to be instant and easy.*

If an adult swimmer is tense, unrelaxed or anxious, the leg and arm movements are usually incomplete and therefore lack the power to assist the body lift. A lack of flexibility will add to this, plus any lack of flexibility in the neck joints will make lifting the head to breathe quite limited.

If you know you don't quite clear the water as you attempt to breathe then human instinct kicks in and you naturally hold your breath and any conscious attempt you make at inhaling results in a mouth full of water.

Despite the frustratingly long time it seems to take to get this right, it is possible to get there. Trust me on this. I've seen adults just like yourself go through the exact same experiences and eventually learn to swim breaststroke and get the hang of breathing to the point that it is like second nature.

How? Learn to swim slowly at first. Take a woggle, place it under your arms and swim breaststroke in slow motion. The extra support will help you clear the water to breath and swimming slowly will firstly allow you time to exhale completely in the water and more importantly help you to relax.

Relaxation leads to increased confidence and increased confidence leads to increased relaxation. It's a not-so vicious circle.

Its very easy when learning to swim to get caught up in swimming a certain distance. Just before you push off from the wall you subconsciously have a goal in mind of how far you need to get. 5m, 10m, whatever it is forget it. The distance you cover is not important.

As you experiment with swimming slowly, or in slow motion you will soon be pleasantly surprised to find yourself covering some distance without really trying. This is because you are learning to feel your way through the water and not fight your way through it. There is a difference and it is this difference that can be hard as well as time consuming to find, but when you do it is like that 'riding a bike' moment."

Chapter 12: Basic Floating Exercises

Discover Your Level Of Buoyancy And Stay Afloat

All of the exercises listed below are designed to help discover your own level of buoyancy and if you are a natural sinker, how fast or slow you actually sink.

Providing you have read the previous parts of this book that explain how to relax, how to glide and how to breathe, you can then use these exercises to help keep your body up and keep it moving.

Wearing swim goggles will help to give you a greater sense of awareness.

Exercise #1: Face Down Floating

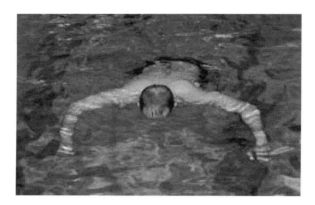

Take a deep breath and submerge your face whilst bringing your legs up to the surface.

Lay face down with arms and legs wide to cover as much surface area as possible. Lay there for as long as you can hold your breath and feel how your body behaves in this stationary position.

You will most probably find your legs slowly sinking first. See how slowly they sink and if there are any small movements that can slow down their rate of sinking or even help them back to the surface.

Maybe perform a very slow breaststroke, feeling your way through the water.

Exercise #2: Push and Glide

 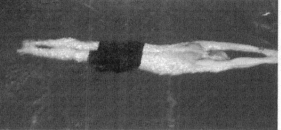

Take a deep breath and push away from the pool wall, face down. Ensure your body is in a stretched out, streamlined position. Glide as far as you can in one breath.

You may find you begin to sink as your momentum slows. See what small movements of the legs, feet and hands are able to keep you moving and afloat.

Feel your way through the water using a gentle breaststroke or front crawl action.

Exercise #3: Push and Glide With Kicks

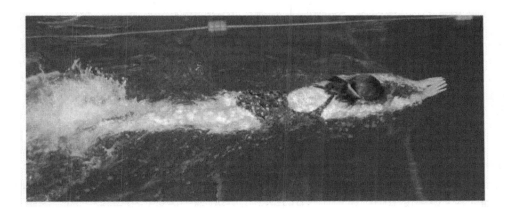

The same exercise as #2 with a push and glide from the poolside. This time add leg kicks to help maintain the momentum and prevent sinking.

The leg kicks can be an alternating kick such the kick used in front crawl, or a simultaneous circular leg kick like the one used for breaststroke.

Exercise #4: Push and Glide On The Back

Perform a push and glide from the poolside in a supine (face up) position. Ensure your head is looking upwards and chest and hips are high up near the water surface. This will help enable the legs and feet to be at or near the water surface too.

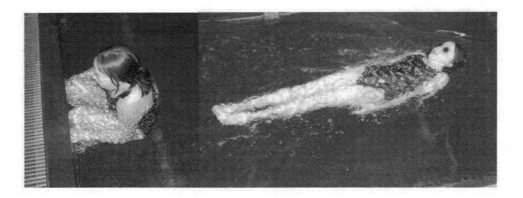

As the glide begins to slow, use the hands by the sides in a sculling type action (using the wrists to help the hands push water towards the feet) under the water and a gentle leg kick to maintain the movement and momentum through the water.

Tips and Tricks

Tip #1
When swimming face up on your front and your legs begin to sink, take a deep breath and put your face down in the water. The act of putting your face into the water can, with some assistance from yourself, encourage your legs to rise again.

Tip #2
When swimming breaststroke use a slightly downward arm pull action. Although breaststroke arm pull is a circular action to help pull through the water, a downwards pull with help to pull the body upwards in the water. This also assists us to breathe as the upper body rises.

Tip #3
Slow down. Swimming slower encourages relaxation, a gliding action and gives us time to breathe, all of which assist us in remaining at the water surface.

Tip #4
Feel your way through the water, don't fight your way through it. Fight the water and it will usually win. Feel you way through it and you will be doing your bit to help the water to support you.

Correct Technique Is The Key

Staying afloat as we swim is all about making our body as efficient as possible as we move through the water. Our body has to cut its way through the water and correct swimming technique is essential for this to happen.

The next few chapters in this book lay out practical exercises and the finer details of how to swim the four basic swimming strokes.

"I wouldn't say anything is impossible. I think that everything is possible as long as you put your mind to it and put the work and time into it."

Michael Phelps - 18 times Olympic Swimming Gold Medalist

Chapter 13: Front Crawl

Basic Front Crawl Technique

Swimming with good front crawl technique is a desire that many long for. Whether its for competition, triathlon or just to feel and look good in your local pool, front crawl is the swimming stroke everyone wants to know how to swim well.

Front crawl is the fastest, most efficient stroke of them all. This is largely down to the streamlined body position and continuous propulsion from the arms and legs.

The alternating action of the arms and legs is relatively easy on the joints and the stroke as a whole develops aerobic capacity faster than any other stroke. In competitive terms it is usually referred to as Freestyle.

The constant alternating arm action generates almost all of the propulsion and is the most efficient arm action of the four basic swimming strokes. The leg action promotes a horizontal, streamlined body position and balances the arm action but provides little propulsion.

Front crawl breathing technique requires the head to be turned so that the mouth clears the water but causes minimal upset to the balance of the body from its normal streamlined position.

The timing and coordination of the arms and legs occur most commonly with six leg kicks to one arm cycle. However, stroke timing can vary, with a four beat cycle and even a two beat cycle, which is most commonly used in long distance swims and endurance events.

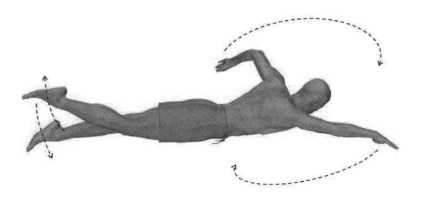

Body Position

The overall body position for front crawl is as streamlined and as flat as possible at the water surface, with the head in-line with the body.

The waterline is around the natural hairline with eyes looking forward and down.

If the position of the head is raised it will cause the position of the hips and legs to lower which in turn will increase frontal resistance, causing the stroke to be inefficient and the breathing technique to be incorrect.

If the head position is too low it will cause the legs to rise and the kick to lose its efficiency.

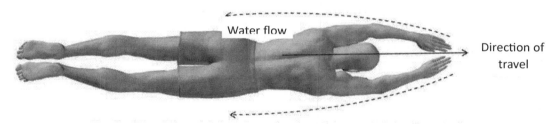

Streamlined body position minimises drag, allowing efficient movement through the water

Shoulders remain at the surface and roll with the arm action. Hips also roll with the stroke technique, close to the water surface and the legs remain in line with the body.

Common Body Position Mistakes

The common body position mistakes made are with head position and hand and feet position during the stroke.

If the head is too high over the water surface, it will cause the legs and feet to be lower under the water surface and cause the overall body position to be angled and therefore very inefficient.

Hands and feet must be together throughout the swimming stroke as this gives the body its streamlined efficiency, allowing it to move smoothly through the water.

If the hands or feet move apart it causes the overall shape of the body in the water to become wider and therefore inefficient.

The best exercise to practice perfecting the correct body position and shape is a push and glide from the poolside. The swimmer pushes off from the pool wall or floor and glides across the water surface, keeping the head central and hands and feet touching together.

Leg Kick

The leg kick for front crawl originates from the hips and both legs kick with equal force.

The legs kick in an up and down alternating action, with the propulsive phase coming from the down kick. There should be a slight bend in the knee due to the water pressure, in order to produce the propulsion required on the down kick.

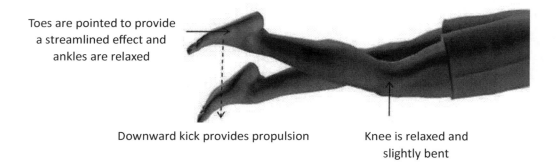

Toes are pointed to provide a streamlined effect and ankles are relaxed

Downward kick provides propulsion

Knee is relaxed and slightly bent

The downward kick begins at the hip and uses the thigh muscles to straighten the leg at the knee, ending with the foot extended to allow it's surface area to bear upon the water. As the leg moves upwards, the sole of the foot and the back of the leg press upwards and backwards against the water.

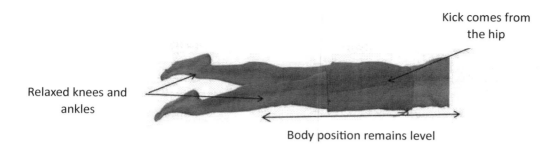

Kick comes from the hip

Relaxed knees and ankles

Body position remains level

The upward kick slows and stops as the leg nears and minimally breaks the water surface. Ankles are relaxed and toes pointed to give an in-toeing effect when kicking and the depth of the kick should be within the overall depth of the body.

Common Leg Kick Mistakes

It is very common to kick from the knees during front crawl, in an attempt to generate some propulsion and movement. This can also lead to a very stiff and robotic kicking action. The kick must originate from the hip and be a smooth movement with relaxed knee and ankle joints.

Another common mistake is to make the kicking movements too large. In other words, the feet come out over the water surface causing excessive splash and again wasting valuable energy.

A good exercise to practice the leg kick is holding a float or a kick board and kicking along the length of the pool with face down. This will allow the swimmer to focus purely on the leg kick, ensuring it is a relaxed and flowing up and down movement.

Arm Action

The continuous alternating arm action provides the majority of the power and propulsion of the entire swimming stroke.

Entry

The hand enters the water at a 45 degree angle; finger tips first, thumb side down. The hand entry should be between the shoulder and head line with a slight elbow bend.

Catch

The hand reaches forward under the water without over stretching and the arm fully extends just under the water surface.

Propulsive Phase

The hand sweeps through the water downwards, inwards and then upwards. The elbow is high at the end of the down sweep and remains high throughout the in-sweep. The hand pulls through towards the thigh and upwards to the water surface.

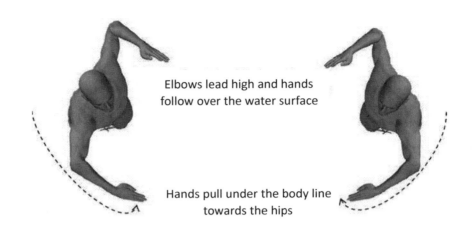

Elbows lead high and hands follow over the water surface

Hands pull under the body line towards the hips

Recovery Phase

The elbow bends to exit the water first. Hand and fingers fully exit the water and follow a straight path along the body-line over the water surface. The elbow is bent and high and the arm is fully relaxed.

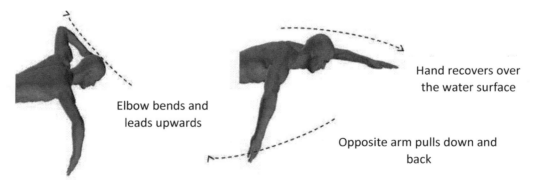

Elbow bends and leads upwards

Hand recovers over the water surface

Opposite arm pulls down and back

Common Arm Technique Mistakes

The arm action can bring about many mistakes, the most common being a deep propulsive phase and a very high recovery phase.

Both of these mistakes will disturb the body position, which will in turn create an inefficient overall swimming stroke. Both a deep arm pull and a high arm recovery over the water surface will also cause excessive body roll.

The best exercise for practicing and correcting these common mistakes is holding a float in one hand and swimming using single arm pulls. This will force the swimmer to focus on the arm technique whilst ensuring that the body position remains level and correct.

Breathing Technique

The head turns to the side on inhalation for front crawl breathing technique. The head begins to turn at the end of the upward arm sweep and turns enough for the mouth to clear the water and inhale. The head turns back into the water just as the arm recovers over and the hand returns to the water. Breathing can be bilateral (alternate sides every one and a half stroke cycles) or unilateral (same side) depending of the stroke cycle and distance to be swum.

Breathe IN as the arm pulls through and the head turns to the side

Types of Breathing Technique

Trickle Breathing

The breath is slowly exhaled through the mouth and nose into the water during the propulsive phase of the arm pull. The exhalation is controlled to allow inhalation to take place easily as the arm recovers.

Explosive Breathing

The breath is held after inhalation during the propulsive arm phase and then released explosively, part in and part out of the water, as the head is turned to the side.

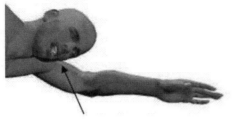

Breathe IN as the head turns
out of the water

Breathe OUT as the head faces
forwards and down

Common Breathing Mistakes

It is very common, especially for beginners, to perform explosive breathing without knowing they are doing so. Holding the breath during the swimming stroke comes naturally to most people but it is not necessarily the most energy efficient way of swimming.

Breath holding causes an increase in carbon dioxide in the system, which increases the urgency to breathe. This can cause swimmers to become breathless very quickly.

Trickle breathing is the most effective breathing technique for beginners as it allows a gentle release of carbon dioxide from the lungs, which then makes inhalation easier.

Another common mistake is to lift the head instead of rolling the head to the side. Lifting the head causes the legs to sink, the body position to be disturbed and the overall swimming stroke to be inefficient.

The best exercise for perfecting trickle breathing and ensuring the head is not lifting, is to hold a float with a diagonal grip and kick. The diagonal grip allows space for the head to roll to the side.

Timing and Coordination

The timing and coordination for front crawl usually occurs naturally.

The arms should provide a powerful propulsive alternating action whilst leg kicks also remain continuous and alternating.

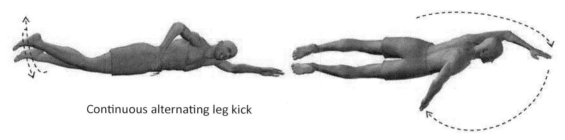

Continuous alternating leg kick

Continuous alternating arm action

What Exactly Is 'Timing'?

When we talk about timing, we usually refer to the number of leg kicks per arm pull cycle. In other words, how many times or legs kick in the time it takes for our arms to complete one arm pull cycle.

Find A Timing Pattern To Suit You

There are three common timing patterns:

• Six Beat cycle

• Four beat cycle

• Two beat cycle

Where one 'beat' refers to one leg kick.

Six beat cycle

Each leg kicks three down kicks per single arm pull, resulting in six kicks per arm cycle. This timing pattern is normally taught to beginners as it comes most naturally. It is also used for sprint swims.

Four beat cycle

Each leg kicks down twice for each arm pull, resulting in four leg kicks per arm pull cycle. Not very common but works for some.

Two-beat cycle

Each leg kicks down once per arm pull, resulting in two kick per arm pull cycle. This timing cycle is normally used by long distance swimmers, where the leg kick acts as a counter balance instead of a source of propulsion.

Although the two-beat cycle is not ideal, some beginners may find it less tiring and the coordination easier.

Common Timing Mistakes

These various timing and coordination cycles bring varying degrees of mistakes, the most common being an attempt to kick too fast.

The required speed of the leg kick and therefore the timing cycle required for the stroke depends on the distance that is to be swum. A long distance swim requires the leg kick to counter balance the arm action, so the two beat cycle is best used. The short sprint requires a faster leg kick so the six beat cycle is needed so that the legs can provide more propulsion.

It is easy to kick with a fast leg kick and unknowingly allow the arm action to also speed up. This results in a loss of arm technique and overall body shape leading to a poor and inefficient swimming stroke.

Catch up is the best swimming exercise to not only establish correct timing and coordination cycle but to experiment with different timing cycles, as the delayed arm action slows down the exercise.

Front Crawl Overview

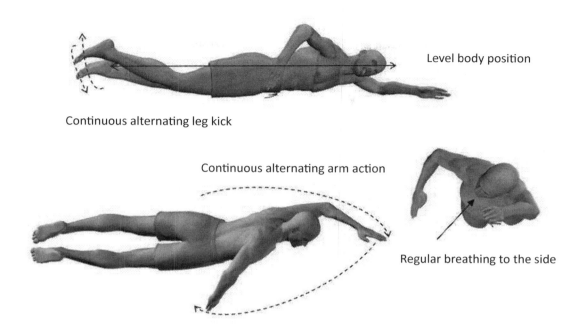

Level body position

Continuous alternating leg kick

Continuous alternating arm action

Regular breathing to the side

Front Crawl Exercises

The next section contains practical exercises to help learn and fine-tune each separate part of your front crawl technique.

They are designed to isolate each stroke part so that you can learn exactly what each part of your body should be doing.

FRONT CRAWL: Body Position

Holding the poolside

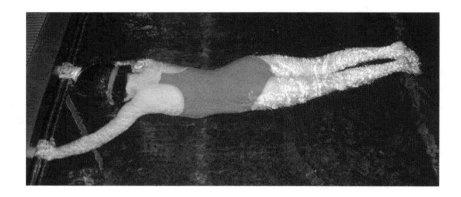

Aim: to encourage confidence in a floating position.

The swimmer holds the poolside for added security and some assistance may be required, as some people will be unable naturally afloat.

Key Actions

- Relax
- Keep the head tucked between the arms
- Stretch out as far as you can
- Keep your feet together

Technical Focus

- Head is central and still

- Face is submerged

- Eyes are looking downwards

- Shoulders should be level

- Hips are close to the surface

- Legs are together and in line with the body

Hands holding the
pool side or rail

Overall body position is as horizontal as possible depending
on the swimmers own buoyancy

Common Faults

- Failure to submerge the face

- Overall body is not relaxed

- Head is not central

- Whole body is not remaining straight

- Feet are not together

FRONT CRAWL: Body Position

Static practice holding floats

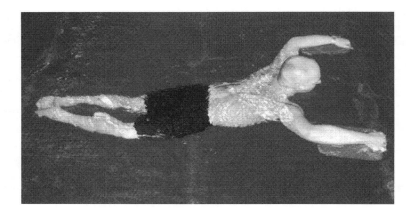

Aim: to help the swimmer develop confidence in their own buoyancy.

A float can be held under each arm or a single float held out in front, depending on levels of confidence and ability. Some swimmers may need extra assistance if they lack natural buoyancy.

Key Actions

- Relax
- Keep the head tucked between the arms
- Stretch out as far as you can
- Keep your feet together

Technical Focus

- Head is central and still
- Face is submerged
- Eyes are looking downwards
- Shoulders should be level
- Hips are close to the surface
- Legs are together and in line with the body

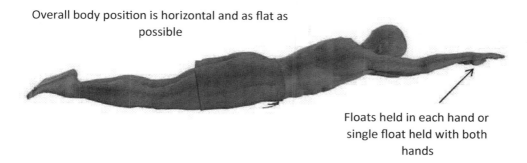

Overall body position is horizontal and as flat as possible

Floats held in each hand or single float held with both hands

Common Faults

- Failure to submerge the face
- Head is not central
- Whole body is not remaining straight
- Feet and hands are not together

FRONT CRAWL: Body Position

Push and glide from standing

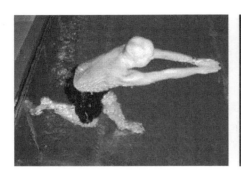 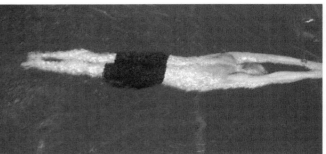

Aim: to develop correct body position and confidence in pushing off.

The swimmer can start with arms stretched out in front and pushes off from the pool floor or from the wall with one foot and glides through the water unaided.

Key Actions

- Push hard from the side/pool floor
- Keep your head tucked between your arms
- Stretch out as far as you can
- Keep your hands together
- Keep your feet together

Technical Focus

- Initial push should be enough to gain good movement

- Head remains still and central

- Face submerged so that the water is at brow level

- Shoulders should be level

- Legs in line with the body

Legs push off from the pool
side or pool floor

Direction of travel

Common Faults

- Failure to submerge the face

- Push off is too weak

- Whole body is not remaining straight

- Feet are not together

FRONT CRAWL: Body Position

Push and glide from the side holding floats

Aim: to develop correct body position whilst moving through the water.

Body position should be laying prone with the head up at this stage. The use of floats helps to build confidence, particularly in the weak or nervous swimmer. The floats create a slight resistance to the glide, but this is still a useful exercise.

Key Actions

- Push hard from the wall
- Relax and float across the water
- Keep your head still and look forward
- Stretch out as far as you can
- Keep your feet together

Technical Focus

- Head remains still and central with the chin on the water surface
- Eyes are looking forwards and downwards
- Shoulders should be level and square
- Hips are close to the surface
- Legs are in line with the body

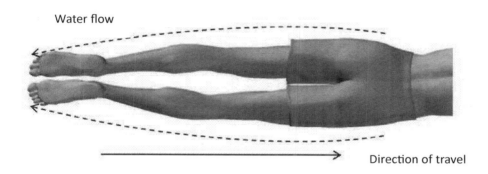

Water flow

Direction of travel

Common Faults

- Push from the side is not hard enough
- Head is not central
- Whole body is not remaining straight
- Feet are not together

FRONT CRAWL: Body Position

Push and glide from the poolside

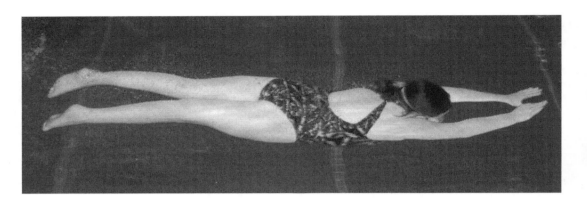

Aim: to develop a streamlined body position whilst moving thorough the water.

Movement is created by pushing and gliding from holding position at the poolside.

Key Actions

• Push hard from the side

• Stretch your arms out in front as you push

• Keep your head tucked between your arms

• Stretch out as far as you can

• Keep your hands and feet together

Technical Focus

- Head remains still and central
- Face submerged so that the water is at brow level
- Shoulders should be level and square
- Legs are in line with the body
- Overall body position should be streamlined

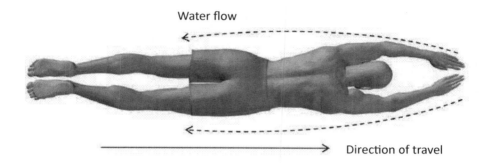

Streamlined body position minimises drag, allowing efficient movement
through the water

Common Faults

- Push off is too weak
- Arms stretch in front after the push
- Head is not central
- Overall body position not in line
- Hands or feet are not together

FRONT CRAWL: Legs

Sitting on the poolside kicking

Aim: to give the swimmer the feel of the water during the kick.

Sitting on poolside kicking is an ideal exercise for the beginner to practise correct leg kicking action with the added confidence of sitting on the poolside.

Key Actions

- Kick with straight legs
- Pointed toes
- Make a small splash with your toes
- Kick with floppy feet
- Kick continuously

Technical Focus

- Kick is continuous and alternating
- Knee is only slightly bent
- Legs are close together when they kick
- Ankles are relaxed and the toes are pointed

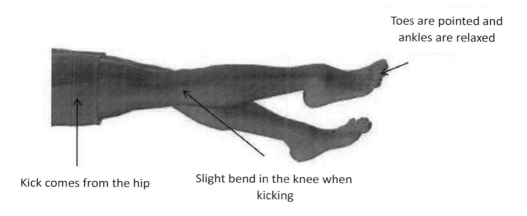

Toes are pointed and ankles are relaxed

Kick comes from the hip

Slight bend in the knee when kicking

Common Faults

- Knees bend too much
- Kick comes from the knee
- Stiff ankles

FRONT CRAWL: Legs

Holding the poolside

Aim: to encourage the swimmer to learn the kicking action.

Holding the poolside enhances confidence and helps develop leg strength and technique.

Key Actions

- Kick with straight legs
- Pointed toes
- Make a small splash with your toes
- Kick with floppy feet
- Kick from your hips
- Kick continuously
- Legs kick close together

Technical Focus

- Kick comes from the hip
- Kick is continuous and alternating
- Knee is only slightly bent
- Legs are close together when they kick
- Ankles are relaxed and the toes are pointed
- Kick should just break the water surface

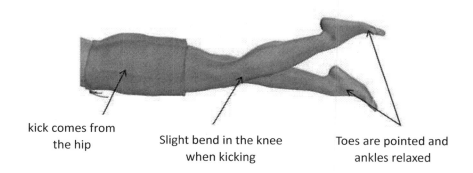

kick comes from the hip

Slight bend in the knee when kicking

Toes are pointed and ankles relaxed

Common Faults

- Feet come out of the water
- Kick comes from the knee
- Legs are too deep in the water

FRONT CRAWL: Legs

Legs kick with a float held under each arm

Aim: to learn correct kicking technique and develop leg strength.

The added stability of two floats will help boost confidence in the weak swimmer.

Key Actions

- Kick with straight legs
- Pointed toes
- Kick with floppy feet
- Kick from your hips
- Kick continuously

Technical Focus

- Kick comes from the hip
- Kick is continuous and alternating
- Chin remains on the water surface
- Legs are close together when they kick
- Ankles are relaxed and the toes are pointed
- Kick should just break the water surface
- Upper body and arms should be relaxed

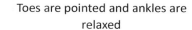

Toes are pointed and ankles are relaxed

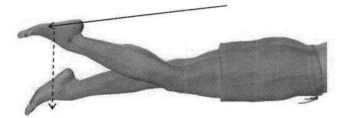

Downward kick provides propulsion

Common Faults

- Head lifts above the surface, causing the legs to sink
- Kick comes from the knee causing excessive bend
- Kick is not deep enough
- Legs are too deep in the water

FRONT CRAWL: Legs

Float held with both hands

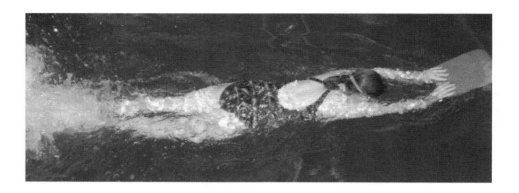

Aim: to practise and learn correct kicking technique.

Holding a float or kickboard out in front isolates the legs, encourages correct body position and develops leg strength.

Key Actions

- Kick with pointed toes
- Make a small splash with your toes
- Kick with floppy feet
- Legs kick close together

Technical Focus

- Kick comes from the hip
- Kick is continuous and alternating.
- Legs are close together when they kick
- Ankles are relaxed and the toes are pointed.
- Kick should just break the water surface.

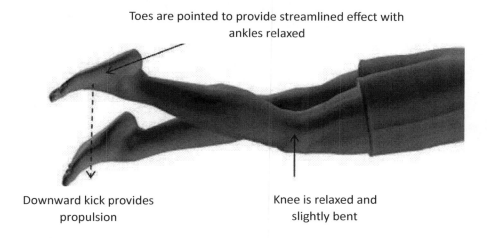

Toes are pointed to provide streamlined effect with
ankles relaxed

Downward kick provides
propulsion

Knee is relaxed and
slightly bent

Common Faults

- Knees bend too much
- Feet come out of the water
- Kick comes from the knee
- Legs are too deep in the water

FRONT CRAWL: Legs

Push and glide with added leg kick

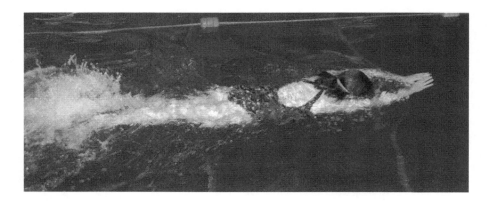

Aim: to develop correct body position and leg kick whilst holding the breath.

Push and glide without a float and add a leg kick whilst maintaining a streamlined body position.

Key Actions

- Kick with straight legs and pointed toes
- Kick with floppy feet
- Kick from your hips
- Kick continuously

Technical Focus

- Kick comes from the hip
- Streamlined body position is maintained
- Kick is continuous and alternating
- Legs are close together when they kick
- Ankles are relaxed and the toes are pointed
- Kick should just break the water surface

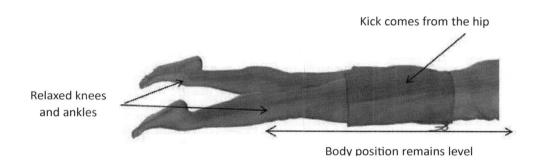

Kick comes from the hip

Relaxed knees and ankles

Body position remains level

Common Faults

- Feet come out of the water
- Stiff ankles
- Kick is not deep enough
- Legs are too deep in the water

FRONT CRAWL: Legs

Leg kick whilst holding a float vertically in front

Aim: to create resistance and help develop strength and stamina.

Holding a float vertically in front increases the intensity of the kicking action, which in turn develops leg strength and stamina.

Key Actions

- Kick with straight legs and pointed toes
- Kick with floppy feet
- Kick from your hips
- Kick continuously

Technical Focus

- Kick comes from the hip
- Streamlined body position is maintained
- Kick is continuous and alternating
- Legs are close together when they kick
- Ankles are relaxed and the toes are pointed
- Kick should just break the water surface

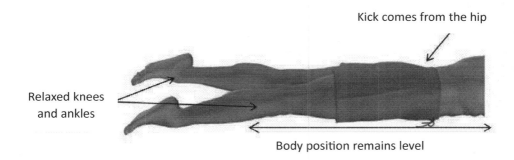

Kick comes from the hip

Relaxed knees and ankles

Body position remains level

Common Faults

- Feet come out of the water
- Stiff ankles
- Kick is not deep enough
- Legs are too deep in the water

FRONT CRAWL: Arms

Standing on the poolside or in shallow water

Aim: to practise correct arm movement whilst in a static position.

This is an exercise for beginners that can be practised on the poolside or standing in shallow water.

Key Actions

- Keep your fingers together
- Continuous smooth action
- Brush your hand past your thigh
- Gradually bend your elbow

Technical Focus

- Fingers should be together

- Pull through to the hips

- Elbow bends and leads upwards

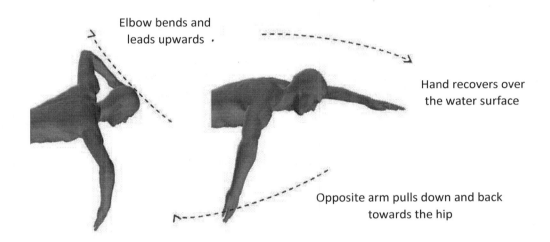

Elbow bends and leads upwards

Hand recovers over the water surface

Opposite arm pulls down and back towards the hip

Common Faults

- Fingers are too wide apart

- Pull is short and not to the thigh

- Arms are too straight as they pull

- Arms are too straight on recovery

- Hand entry is wide of the shoulder line

FRONT CRAWL: Arms

Single arm practice with float held in one hand

Aim: to practise and improve correct arm technique

This practice allows the swimmer to develop arm technique whilst maintaining body position and leg kick. Holding a float with one hand gives the weaker swimmer security and allows the competent swimmer to focus on a single arm.

Key Actions

- Keep your fingers together
- Brush your hand past your thigh
- Pull fast under the water
- Make an 'S' shape under the water
- Elbow out first
- Reach over the water surface

Technical Focus

- Fingertips enter first with thumb side down
- Fingers should be together
- Pull should be an elongated 'S' shape
- Pull through to the hips
- Elbow exits the water first
- Fingers clear the water on recovery

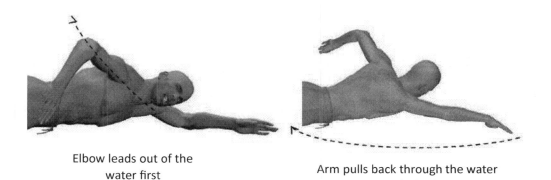

Elbow leads out of the
water first

Arm pulls back through the water
towards the hip

Common Faults

- Fingers are apart
- Pull is short and not to the thigh
- Lack of power in the pull
- Arm pull is too deep underwater
- Arms are too straight on recovery

FRONT CRAWL: Arms

Alternating arm pull whilst holding a float out in front

Aim: to develop coordination and correct arm pull technique.

The swimmer uses an alternating arm action. This also introduces a timing aspect, as the leg kick has to be continuous at the same time.

Key Actions

- Finger tips in first
- Brush your hand past your thigh
- Pull fast under the water
- Elbow out first
- Reach over the water surface

Technical Focus

- Clean entry with fingertips first and thumb side down
- Fingers should be together
- Each arm pulls through to the hips
- Elbow leads out first
- Fingers clear the water on recovery

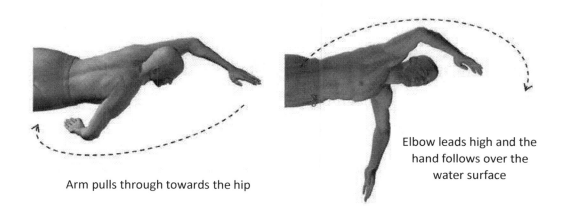

Arm pulls through towards the hip

Elbow leads high and the hand follows over the water surface

Common Faults

- Fingers are too wide apart
- Pull is short and not to the thigh
- Lack of power in the pull
- Arms are too straight on recovery
- Hand entry is wide of shoulder line

FRONT CRAWL: Arms

Arm action using a pull-buoy

Aim: to develop arm pull strength, technique and coordination.

This is a more advanced exercise, which requires stamina and a degree of breathing technique.

Key Actions

- Long strokes
- Smooth continuous action
- Brush your hand past your thigh
- Make an 'S' shape under the water
- Elbow out first
- Reach over the water surface

Technical Focus

- Fingertips enter first with thumb side down

- Fingers should be together

- Pull should be an elongated 'S' shape

- Pull through to the hips

- Elbow comes out first

- Fingers clear the water on recovery

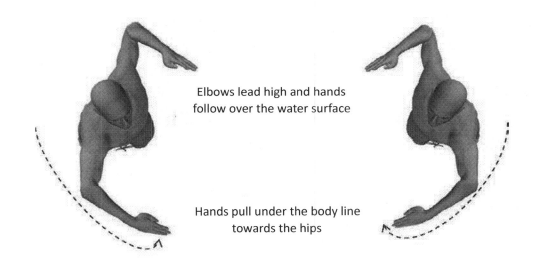

Elbows lead high and hands follow over the water surface

Hands pull under the body line towards the hips

Common Faults

- Pull is short and not to the thigh

- Lack of power in the pull

- Arms pull too deep under water

- Arms are too straight on recovery

- Hand entry is across the centre line

FRONT CRAWL: Arms

Push and glide adding arm cycles

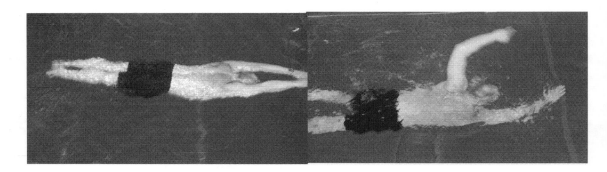

Aim: to combine correct arm action with a streamlined body position.

The swimmer performs a push and glide to establish body position and then adds arm cycles, whilst maintaining body position.

Key Actions

- Finger tips in the water first
- Brush your hand past your thigh
- Make an 'S' shape under the water
- Elbow out first
- Reach over the water surface

Technical Focus

- Clean entry with fingertips first
- Pull should be an elongated 'S' shape
- Pull through to the hips
- Elbow comes out first
- Fingers clear the water on recovery

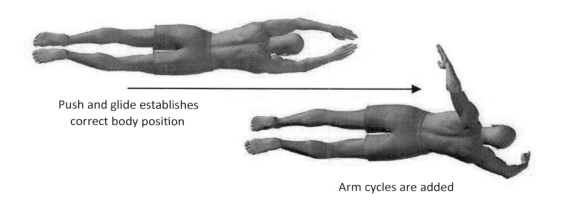

Push and glide establishes
correct body position

Arm cycles are added

Common Faults

- Pull is short and not to the thigh
- Lack of power in the pull
- Arms are too straight under water
- Arms are too straight on recovery
- Hand entry is across centre line

FRONT CRAWL: Breathing

Standing and holding the poolside

Aim: to practice and develop breathing technique.

The pupil stands and holds the pool rail with one arm extended, breathing to one side to introduce the beginner to breathing whilst having his/her face submerged.

Key Actions

- Breathe out through your mouth
- Blow out slowly and gently
- Turn your head to the side when you breathe in
- See how long you can make the breath last

Technical Focus

- Breathing should be from the mouth
- Breathing in should be when the head is turned to the side
- Breathing out should be when the face is down

Breathe IN

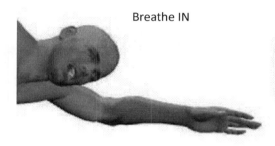

Head turns to the side and mouth clears
the water surface

Breathe OUT

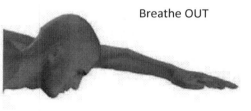

Head faces forwards and down

Common Faults

- Breathing through the nose
- Holding the breath

FRONT CRAWL: Breathing

Holding a float in front with diagonal grip

Aim: to encourage correct breathing technique whilst kicking.

The float is held in front; one arm extended fully, the other holding the near corner with elbow low. This creates a gap for the head and mouth to be turned in at the point of breathing.

Key Actions

• Turn head towards the bent arm to breathe

• Breathe out through your mouth

• Blow out slowly and gently

• Return head to the centre soon after breathing

Technical Focus

- Breathing should be from the mouth
- Breathing in should be when the head is turned to the side
- Breathing out should be slow and controlled

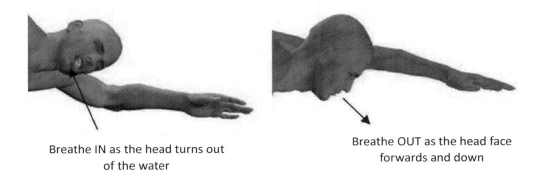

Breathe IN as the head turns out
of the water

Breathe OUT as the head face
forwards and down

Common Faults

- Breathing through the nose
- Holding the breath
- Lifting the head and looking forward when breathing
- Turning towards the straight arm

FRONT CRAWL: Breathing

Float held in one hand, arm action with breathing

Aim: to develop correct breathing technique whilst pulling with one arm.

This allows the swimmer to add the arm action to the breathing technique and perfect the timing of the two movements. The float provides support and keeps the exercise as a simple single arm practice.

Key Actions

- Turn head to the side of the pulling arm
- Breathe out through your mouth
- Blow out slowly and gently
- Return head to the centre soon after breathing

Technical Focus

- Head moves enough for mouth to clear the water
- Breathing in occurs when the head is turned to the side
- Breathing out should be slow
- Breathing should be from the mouth

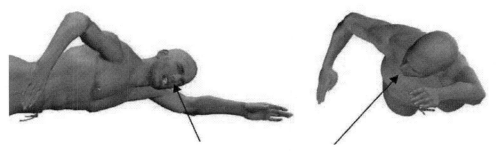

Breathe IN as the arm pulls through and the head turns to the side

Common Faults

- Turning towards the straight arm
- Turning the head too much
- Breathing through the nose
- Holding the breath
- Lifting the head and looking forward when breathing

FRONT CRAWL: Breathing

Float held in both hands, alternate arm pull with breathing

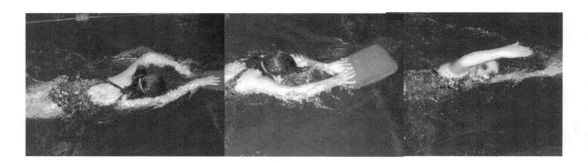

Aim: to practise bi-lateral breathing with the support of a float held out in front.

A single float is held in both hands and one arm pull is performed at a time with the head turning to breathe with each arm pull. Different arm action and breathing cycles can be used, for example; breathe every other arm pull or every three arm pulls.

Key Actions

- Keep head still until you need to breathe
- Breathe every 3 strokes (or another pattern you may choose)
- Turn head to the side as your arm pulls back
- Return head to the centre soon after breathing
- Breathe out through your mouth

Technical Focus

- Head should be still when not taking a breath
- Head movement should be minimal enough for mouth to clear the water
- Breathing in should be when the head is turned to the side
- Breathing should be from the mouth

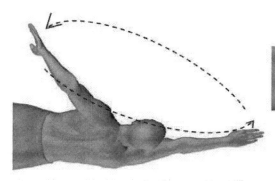 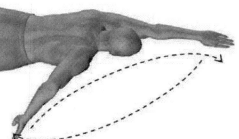

Head turns to the left side as the left arm
pulls through and begins to recover

Head turns to the right side as the right arm
pulls through and begins to recover

Common Faults

- Turning towards the straight arm
- Turning the head too much
- Turning the head too early or late to breath
- Lifting the head and looking forward when breathing

FRONT CRAWL: Timing

Front crawl catch up

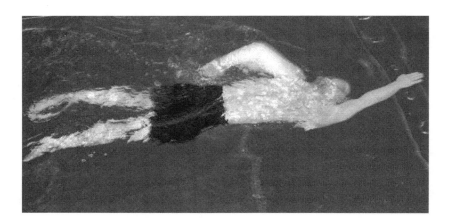

Aim: to practice correct stroke timing and develop coordination.

The opposite arm remains stationary until the arm performing the pull recovers to its starting position. This is an advanced exercise and encourages the swimmer to maintain body position and leg kick whilst practicing arm cycles.

Key Actions

- Finger tips in the water first
- Brush your hand past your thigh
- Make an 'S' shape under the water
- Elbow out first
- Reach over the water surface

Technical Focus

- Clean entry with fingertips first
- Pull should be an elongated 'S' shape
- Pull through to the hips
- Elbow comes out first
- Fingers clear the water on recovery

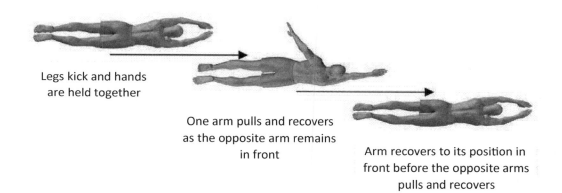

Legs kick and hands are held together

One arm pulls and recovers as the opposite arm remains in front

Arm recovers to its position in front before the opposite arms pulls and recovers

Common Faults

- One leg kick per arm pull
- Continuous leg kick but not enough arm pulls
- Arm pull is too irregular

FRONT CRAWL

Full stroke

Aim: full stroke Front Crawl demonstrating correct leg action, arm action, breathing and timing.

Key Actions

- Keep your head still until you breathe
- Kick continuously from your hips
- Stretch forward with each arm action
- Pull continuously under your body
- Count 3 leg kicks with each arm pull

Technical Focus

- Stroke is smooth and continuous
- Head in line with the body
- Legs in line with the body
- Head remains still
- Leg kick is continuous and alternating
- Arm action is continuous and alternating
- Breathing is regular and to the side
- Stroke ideally has a 6 beat cycle

Common Faults

- Head moves from side to side
- Legs kick from the knee
- Leg action is too slow
- Arm action is untidy and splashing
- Excessive head movement when breathing o Head is lifted, causing legs to sink
- Stroke is erratic and rushed

Real Front Crawl Questions

"When I swim front crawl I have to hold my breath, because my head does not come out of the water enough for me to catch any air. What am I doing wrong?"

Mark's answer:

"Firstly the fact that you are holding your breath in the first place can sometimes cause problems. If you hold your breath you have only a split second to breathe out and then in again, which can be very difficult. So much so that pupils I have taught in the past turn their head as if to breathe but continue to hold their breath.

It could be that your mouth is clearing the water enough to breathe but you are involuntarily continuing to hold your breath.

To overcome this you must breathe out into the water whilst swimming and then when you turn your head to breathe, you only have to breathe in. This makes breathing easier and more relaxed.

If as you suspect the problem is your head not clearing the water surface enough then we need to look at the basics of the breathing technique.

Firstly front crawl breathing technique involves rolling the head to one side and not lifting the head to face forward. Lifting your head upwards will result in that sinking feeling and your mouth will almost certainly not clear the water enough to breathe in.

Ensure that at the point where you roll your head to the side to breathe, your arm on that side must have pulled back to clear a space for your head to turn into. You must then breathe in just as your arm recovers over the water surface.

To ensure that your head rolls to the side enough try looking at your shoulder as you do it. This will ensure you are actually rolling your head and not lifting it. It will also help your mouth to clear the water so that you can breathe.

If you are still struggling try to exaggerate your movement by rolling your head to look at the ceiling above you. Your arm recovery will have to be very high in order to achieve this but it will almost certainly allow you to breathe. However, this is of course technically incorrect but the exaggerated movement will allow you to practice the movement and become confident with breathing. It is therefore important to readjust the technique once you have become proficient by rolling the head the minimum amount so as not to disturb your overall body position."

"How do I coordinate the arms and legs for front crawl? I am just learning to swim and when swimming my arms and my legs will not move in time with each other."

Mark's answer:

"The problem you are referring to is related to your coordination.

Front crawl is an alternating stroke. In other words as one arm pulls the other recovers and as one leg kicks downwards the other kicks upwards.

Unlike breaststroke which is a simultaneous swimming stroke where both arms pull at the same time and both legs also kick at the same time.

You will find that your coordination will favour one more than the other because one will come more naturally than the other.

The timing and coordination of front crawl arms and legs is not something that comes naturally to some people but there is no reason why it cannot be learnt.

A simple exercise to try out is front crawl 'catch up'. Hold a float or kick board with both hands and kick your legs. Then perform one arm pull at a time, taking hold of the float after each complete arm action. You are therefore performing front crawl arms one at a time whilst attempting to maintain your leg kick. Holding the float will help you to focus on your leg kick whilst using your arms.

As for how fast to kick your legs, there is no right or wrong here. The 6 beat cycle is the most traditional where there are 6 leg kicks to each arm cycle (there are 2 arm pulls to a cycle). A 4 beat cycle is also a common pattern and a 1 beat cycle is one of the most common.

Keep in mind that most of the power to generate the movement for front crawl comes from the arms and the legs are there mainly to balance or provide a small amount of power.

For this reason a 2 beat cycle can be quite effective especially as kicking the legs at faster speeds can be very tiring. One leg kicks and one arm pulls.

What you have described is very common and with some practice you will soon have a respectful front crawl swimming stroke."

"I seem to lose my front crawl technique and my kicking when I get tired. The first few lengths are ok but after that when I get tired it's all gone."

Mark's answer:

"Losing your technique because of tiredness is very common and as front crawl is high energy consuming swimming stroke, it doesn't take long before it all falls apart. To be honest 10 lengths is not bad going.

A couple of things to think about that might help you out.

Firstly you mentioned you kicking. Be mindful of how much kicking you are actually doing. It is very common to kick far more than you really need to, especially over a long distance.

Remember the power and propulsion for front crawl comes mainly from the arm action. Propulsion is generated from the leg kick but no way near as much as from the arms.

Watch a long distance front crawl swimmer, for example a triathlete. Each leg kicks once for every arm pull, serving less as propulsion and more as a counter balance to the arm actions, to help keep the whole stroke balanced and even.

On the other hand take a short distance front crawl sprint, over 50 or 100 meters. The legs kick with enormous speed and power to provide maximum propulsion and assistance to the arms with this short distance using up all energy.

Conclusion: less leg kicks equals energy saved - energy that you will need in order to swim a longer distance.

Secondly be mindful of your breathing and in particular how often you breathe. Ensure that you exhale into the water (the easiest and most natural method) and not hold your breath, as this only serves to make you more tired.

Once again the distance being swum will dictate the frequency that you need to breathe. Longer distances more often and shorter distances less. This may sound obvious but it is all too easy to set off from the start and get the pace and frequency of the breathing wrong, despite what might feel right at the time, only for it to catch you out later in the swim.

Breathing every stroke or every other stroke will help to keep a steady pace and hopefully allow you to last longer. Bilateral breathing (alternating the side you breathe to by taking a breath every three arm pulls) is a nice even and steady breathing pattern.

However even this cannot be maintained over long distances. Taking a breath every stroke cycle will cover longer distances, which again you will see if you watch any long distance swimmer.

Lastly there is the age-old problem of fitness. Your fitness and stamina will ultimately dictate how far you can swim before your body tells you it has had enough. Like any form of exercise, the more you do it the fitter and stronger you become."

Chapter 14: Backstroke

Basic Backstroke Technique

This is the most efficient stroke swum on the back and is the third fastest of all swimming strokes. The majority of the power is produced by the alternating arm technique and its horizontal streamlined body position gives it its efficiency. Therefore this is the preferred stroke in competitive races swum on the back.

The nature of floating on the back, face up (supine) can be a calming and relaxing feeling. Also the face is clear of the water, allowing easy breathing and little water splashes onto the face. On the other hand it can be counter productive at first, as it can give a feeling of disorientation and unease, as the swimmer is facing upwards and therefore unaware of their surroundings. The supine body position is flat and horizontal, with ears slightly below the water surface.

The legs kick in an alternating action, continuously up and down to help balance the action of the arms. This stroke has two different arm actions: the bent arm pull, which is the most efficient, and the straight arm pull, which is the easiest to learn. Therefore the straight arm pull is best for beginners.

Breathing should be in time with recovery of each arm, breathing in with one arm recovery and out with the other. Ideally there should be 6 leg kicks to one arm cycle but the stroke timing may vary according to the swimmer's level of coordination.

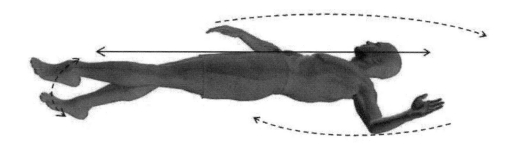

Body Position

The supine body position for this stroke is flat and horizontal, with ears slightly below the water surface.

Good floaters will find this position relaxing and relatively easy, whereas poor floaters will find it difficult to achieve a comfortable head position.

Body position remains horizontal and relaxed

The head remains still throughout the stroke with the eyes looking slightly down the body at a point the swimmer is swimming away from.

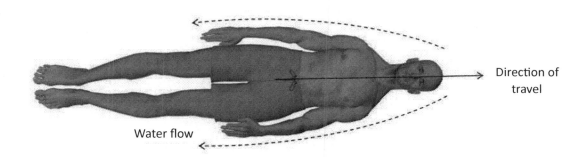

The head position is important because a raised head makes it more difficult to keep the hips raised in the correct position, which leads to a sitting type position in the water.

The hips and shoulders remain at or near the water surface but roll with the stroke. The legs and feet should be extended and remain together to maximise efficiency, with knees remaining below the water surface.

Common Body Position Mistakes

Ever get that feeling that you are sinking when you swim on your back? It is very common to allow the legs to drop and the body position to become angled in the water without knowing it is happening. This is usually caused either by allowing the hips to drop or lifting the head slightly or a combination of both. As the legs drop deeper the whole stroke becomes less efficient and more energy consuming.

Performing a push and glide from holding the poolside is a good way of testing how flat you can remain. Ensure that you look upwards as you push away and stretch out so that your hips, legs and feet rise to the surface. The overall body position is easily maintained with a correct and efficient leg kick.

Leg Kick

During this stroke the legs kick in an alternating action, continuously up and down to help balance the action of the arms.

Legs should be stretched out with toes pointed (plantar flexed) and ankles should be relaxed and loose with toes pointing slightly inwards.

The amount of propulsion generated from the kick will depend on the size of the feet, ankle mobility and strength of the legs.

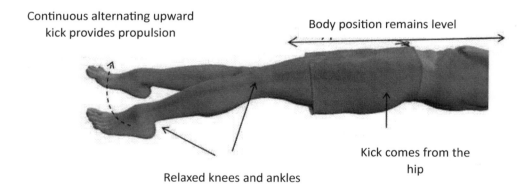

Continuous alternating upward kick provides propulsion

Body position remains level

Relaxed knees and ankles

Kick comes from the hip

The knee should bend slightly and then straighten as the leg kicks upwards. Toes should kick to create a small splash but not break the water surface.

During specific leg practices the legs kick in a vertical plane. However, the arm action causes the body to roll making the legs kick part sideways, part vertical and partly to the other side.

Common Leg Kick Mistakes

The most common fault with the leg kick during backstroke is closely related to the body position, when the swimmer allows their legs to sink below the water surface. The toes should just break the water surface and the legs kick from the hip with a slight bend at the knee.

An easy exercise to help maintain leg kick technique at the correct level in the water is to hold a float or kick board across the chest and perform the leg kick. The float will provide support so that the swimmer can focus on kicking up towards the water surface whilst maintaining a level head and level hips. Only then will the leg kick be at its most efficient.

Arm Action

There are two possible arm actions for backstroke. The bent arm pull, which is more effective because it is faster and has greater propulsion, and the straight arm pull used in more recreational backstroke.

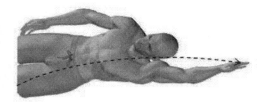

Arm rises upwards, little finger leading and arm brushing the ear

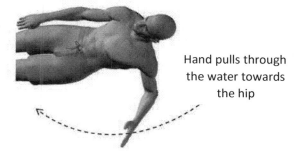

Hand pulls through the water towards the hip

Straight Arm Pull

Entry
The arm should be straight and as inline with the shoulder as possible. The hand should be turned with palm facing outwards and little finger entering the water first.

Propulsive Phase
The arm sweeps through the water in a semi-circle, pulling with force just under the water surface, pulling to the outside of the thigh.

Recovery

The thumb or the back of the hand should exit the water first. The shoulders roll again with the shoulder of the recovering arm rolling upwards. The arm rotates through 180 degrees over the shoulder. The palm is turned outwards during recovery to ensure that the hand enters the water little finger first.

Bent Arm Pull

As the arm pulls through to completion, the overall path should follow an 'S' shape.

Entry

The entry is the same as the straight arm pull, with the little finger entering first, the palm facing out and the arm close to the shoulder line.

Downward Sweep

The palm should always face the direction of travel. The shoulders roll and the elbow bends slightly as the arm sweeps downwards and outwards.

Upwards Sweep

As the hand sweeps inline with the shoulder, the palm changes pitch to sweep upwards and inwards. The elbow should then bend to 90 degrees and point to the pool floor.

Second Downward Sweep

The arm action then sweeps inwards towards the thigh and the palm faces downwards. The bent arm action is completed with the arm fully extended and the hand pushing downwards to counter balance the shoulder roll.

Recovery

The thumb or the back of the hand should exit the water first. The shoulders roll again with the shoulder of the recovering arm rolling upwards. The arm rotates through 180 degrees over the shoulder. The palm is turned outwards during recovery to ensure that the hand enters the water little finger first.

Common Arm Pull Mistakes

Two common faults cause the arm technique for backstroke to become weak and the overall stroke inefficient.

Firstly the upper arm must brush past the ear and the edge of the hand must enter the water in line with the shoulder. If the hand enters the water wide of the shoulder line then the arm pull will be incomplete and lack power.

Secondly it is very common to perform one arm pull at a time. In other words one arm completes a full arm pull cycle before the second arm begins its arm cycle. The arm pulls for backstroke should be continuous where one arm begins to pull as the other arm begins to recover.

Practicing the arm technique whilst holding a float on the chest is a good way of ensuring the hand is entering inline with the shoulder and that the arm pull is complete. Once this has been mastered then the swimmer can practice the full stroke ensuring the arms are performing continuous cycles.

Breathing

Breathing during backstroke should be relaxed and easy, due to the supine body position and face being out of the water throughout the stroke. Most swimmers are neither aware of the way in which they breathe, nor the pattern of breathing or point at which a breath is taken.

Breathing should be in time with the recovery of each arm, breathing in with one arm recovery and out with the other. This encourages a breath to be taken at regular intervals.

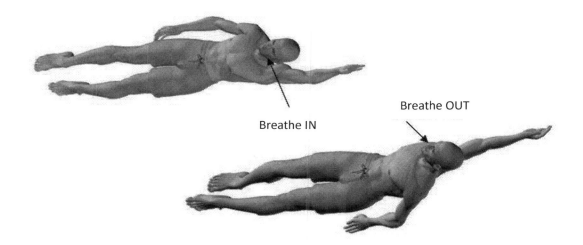

Breathe IN

Breathe OUT

A regular breathing pattern should be encouraged to prevent breath holding, particularly in beginners.

Common Breathing Mistakes

Breath holding is a common mistake made when swimming this stroke and the result is a very tired and breathless swimmer. Do you ever feel like you become breathless very quickly when swimming this stroke? It goes without saying that swimming contains a very large element of fitness and stamina but this is only one factor.

Breathing technique is essential and it is very common for swimmers, especially beginners to hold their breath without knowing they are doing so.

Performing the stroke slowly at first or with floats to provide support, swimmers must breathe out and then in again in time with each arm pull. Try to establish a rhythm of breathing through each stroke cycle and this will help to prevent breath holding and unnecessary tiredness and exhaustion.

An established breathing rhythm will help to maintain the timing and coordination of the arms and legs as they pull and kick. It will also assist the swimmer to relax and therefore swim with a calm, controlled and smooth backstroke.

Timing and Coordination

The timing and coordination of the arms and legs develops with practice.

Ideally there should be 6 leg kicks to one arm cycle. The opposite leg kicks downwards at the beginning of each arm pull. This helps to balance the body. This may vary according to the swimmer's level of coordination.

One arm exists the water as the other begins to pull and the
leg kick remains continuous

Arm action should be continuous. i.e. when one arm enters and begins to pull, the other should begin its recovery phase.

Common Timing Mistakes

A common mistake is performing one arm cycle at a time, resulting in an uneven and unbalanced stroke overall.

Timing and coordination problems occur with backstroke when the legs are allowed to sink below the water surface and the arms lose their continuity and pull one arm at a time.

Counting in your head can sometimes help to maintain stroke rhythm and timing. If you are able to perform a 6 beat cycle then you should count to 3 during each arm pull, therefore kicking 3 legs kicks per arm pull.

If a one beat cycle comes more naturally then there should be one leg kick for each arm pull. Performing the stroke slowly at first will help to establish the rhythm and timing and only when you are proficient swimming at a slow steady pace should you try to increase speed.

With increases in speed comes the greater potential for the timing and coordination to become disrupted and the overall swimming stroke to lose it efficiency.

Backstroke Overview

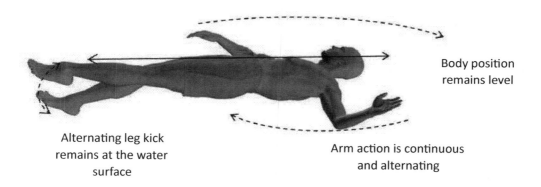

Body position
remains level

Alternating leg kick
remains at the water
surface

Arm action is continuous
and alternating

Backstroke Exercises

The next section contains practical exercises to help learn and fine-tune each separate part of your backstroke technique.

They are designed to isolate each stroke part so that you can learn exactly what each part of your body should be doing.

BACKSTROKE: Body Position

Floating supine supported by floats

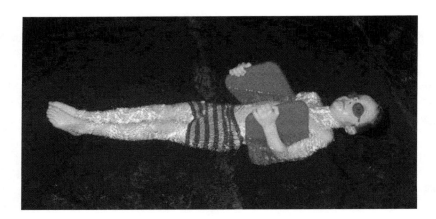

Aim: to gain confidence in a supine position on the water surface.

This exercise is ideal for the nervous swimmer. The teacher or assistant initially can provide support, if he/she is also in the water. 2 floats can then provide support, one placed under each arm, or by a woggle placed under both arms as in the photograph above.

Key Actions

- Relax

- Make your body flat on top of the water

- Keep your head back

- Push your tummy up to the surface

- Look up to the ceiling

- Keep your head still

- Keep yourself in a long straight line

Technical Focus

- Overall body should be horizontal and streamlined
- Head remains still
- Eyes looking upwards and towards the feet
- Hips must be close to the surface
- Legs must be together

Body position remains level

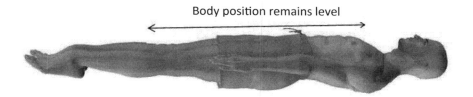

Common Faults

- Head raises out of the water
- Tummy and hips sink
- Failing to maintain a flat position

BACKSTROKE: Body Position

Static supine position, holding a single float

Aim: to develop confidence in a supine position.

Holding a single float across the chest gives security to the nervous swimmer, but is not as stable as a woggle or a float under each arm and so is a subtle and gradual progression. If necessary, this exercise can be performed without a float, as shown in the diagram below, as an additional progression.

Key Actions

- Relax
- Keep your head back
- Push your tummy up to the surface
- Look up to the ceiling
- Keep your head still

Technical Focus

- Overall body should be horizontal

- Head remains still

- Eyes looking upwards

- Hips must be close to the surface

- Legs must be together

Body position remains horizontal and relaxed

Common Faults

- Head raises out of the water

- Eyes look up but head tips forward

- Tummy and hips sink

- Head moves about

- Failing to maintain a straight line

BACKSTROKE: Body Position

Push and glide holding a float

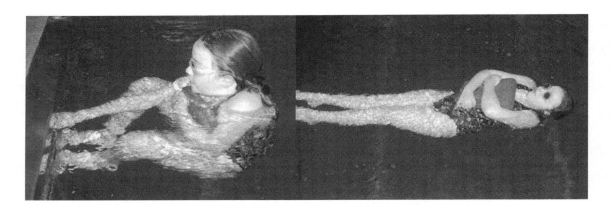

Aim: to gain confidence and move through the water in a supine position.

Holding a float gives added security to the nervous or weak swimmer whilst helping to maintain correct body position.

Key Actions

- Relax
- Keep your head back and chin up
- Push your tummy up to the surface
- Look up to the ceiling
- Keep your head still
- Push off like a rocket

Technical Focus

- Overall body should be horizontal and streamlined
- Head remains still
- Eyes looking upwards
- Hips must be close to the surface
- Legs must be together

Body position remains level

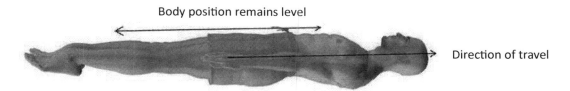

Direction of travel

Float can be placed on the chest or behind the head as in the photos above

Common Faults

- Head raises out of the water
- Eyes look up but head tips forward
- Tummy and hips sink
- Head moves about
- Failing to maintain a straight line

BACKSTROKE: Body Position

Push and glide from the poolside without floats

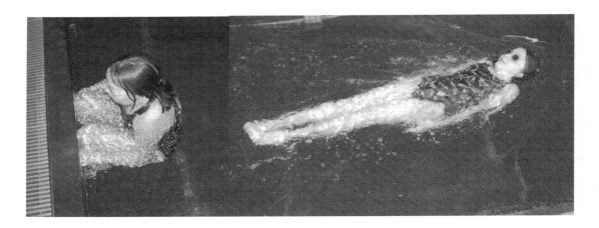

Aim: to encourage correct body position whilst moving.

The swimmer uses the momentum of a push from the poolside. Arms are held by the sides or held straight over the head in more advanced cases.

Key Actions

- Relax

- Make your body as long as you can

- Push off like a rocket

- Push your tummy up to the surface

- Look up to the ceiling

- Glide in a long straight line

Technical Focus

- Overall body should be horizontal and streamlined
- Head remains still
- Eyes looking upwards and towards the feet
- Hips must be close to the surface
- Legs must be together
- Arms are held by the sides

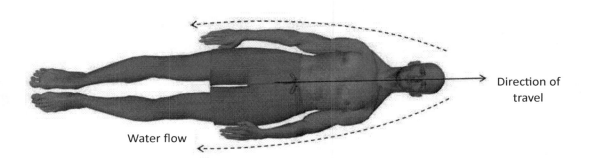

Water flow

Direction of travel

Common Faults

- Push off is not hard enough
- Head raises out of the water
- Tummy and hips sink
- Failing to maintain a straight line

BACKSTROKE: Legs

Static practice, sitting on the poolside

Aim: to develop an alternating leg kick action.

The swimmer is positioned sitting on the poolside with feet in the water. This is ideal for the nervous beginner to get accustomed to the 'feel' of the water.

Key Actions

- Point your toes like a ballerina
- Kick from your hips
- Kick with floppy feet
- Keep your legs together
- Make your legs as long as possible

Technical Focus

- Kick comes from the hips
- Toes are pointed
- Legs are together
- Slight knee bend
- Ankles are relaxed

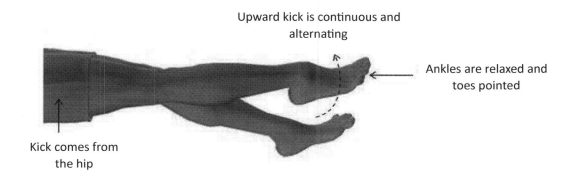

Upward kick is continuous and alternating

Ankles are relaxed and toes pointed

Kick comes from the hip

Common Faults

- Kick comes from the knee
- Legs kick apart
- Toes are turned up
- Legs are too 'stiff', not relaxed

BACKSTROKE: Legs

Woggle held under the arms

Aim: to practise and develop correct leg kick action.

This exercise is ideal for the nervous beginner as an introduction to swimming on the back. The stability of the woggle encourages kicking and motion backwards with ease.

Key Actions

• Point your toes like a ballerina

• Kick from your hips

• Kick with floppy feet

• Make a small splash with your toes

Technical Focus

- Kick comes from the hips

- Kick is alternating and continuous

- Kick breaks the water surface

- Hips and tummy up near the surface

- Toes are pointed and ankles relaxed

- Legs are together

- Slight knee bend

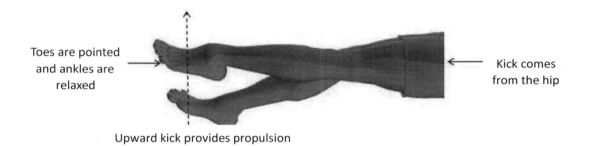

Toes are pointed and ankles are relaxed

Kick comes from the hip

Upward kick provides propulsion

Common Faults

- Kick comes from the knee

- Hips sink and legs kick too deep

- Toes are turned up

- Stiff ankles

- Legs are too 'stiff', not relaxed

BACKSTROKE: Legs

Float held under each arm

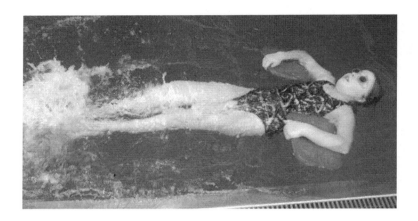

Aim: to practise and develop leg action whilst maintaining correct body position.

Two floats provide good support and encourage a relaxed body position, without creating excessive resistance through the water.

Key Actions

- Relax and kick hard
- Point your toes like a ballerina
- Kick from your hips
- Kick with floppy feet
- Make a small splash with your toes
- Keep your legs together

Technical Focus

- Kick breaks the water surface
- Hips and tummy are up near the surface
- Toes are pointed and ankles relaxed
- Legs are together
- Slight knee bend
- Ankles are relaxed

Body alignment and direction of travel

Continuous alternating upward kick
provides propulsion through the water

Common Faults

- Toes are turned up, causing a lack of motion
- Head comes up, causing legs to sink
- Hips sink and legs kick too deep
- Legs kick apart

BACKSTROKE: Legs

Float held on the chest

Aim: to allow the correct body position to be maintained whilst the legs kick.

This is a progression from having a float held under each arm. The swimmer is less stable but still has the security of one float held on the chest.

Key Actions

- Point your toes like a ballerina
- Kick from your hips
- Kick with floppy feet
- Make a small splash with your toes
- Keep your legs together

Technical Focus

- Kick comes from the hips

- Kick is alternating and continuous

- Kick breaks the water surface

- Hips and tummy up near the surface

- Legs are together

- Ankles are relaxed and toes pointed

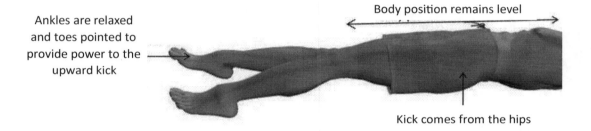

Ankles are relaxed and toes pointed to provide power to the upward kick

Body position remains level

Kick comes from the hips

Common Faults

- Kick comes from the knee o Legs are too deep

- Toes are turned up

- Stiff ankles

- Legs are too 'stiff', not relaxed

BACKSTROKE: Legs

Float held behind the head

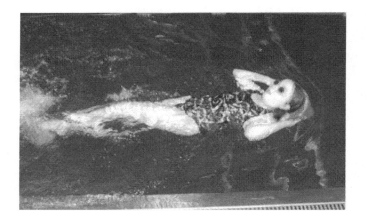

Aim: to encourage correct body position as the legs kick.

The float behind the head helps to keep the chest and hips high. A variation of the exercise with the float held on the chest, this exercise helps to develop leg strength and stamina.

Key Actions

- Kick from your hips

- Kick with floppy feet

- Make a small splash with your toes

- Keep your legs together

Technical Focus

- Kick comes from the hips
- Kick breaks the water surface
- Hips and tummy up near the surface
- Toes are pointed and ankles relaxed
- Legs are together

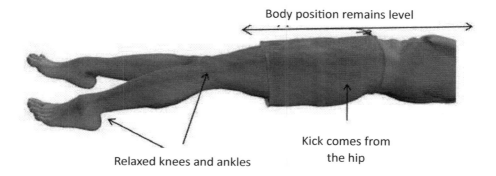

Body position remains level

Relaxed knees and ankles

Kick comes from the hip

Common Faults

- Kick comes from the knee
- Legs are too deep
- Toes are turned up
- Stiff ankles
- Legs too 'stiff', not relaxed

BACKSTROKE: Legs

Float held over the knees

Aim: to prevent excessive knee bend by holding a float over the knees.

This kicking practice should be performed with the float held on the water surface without the knees hitting it as they kick.

Key Actions

- Kick with straight legs
- Point your toes like a ballerina
- Stop your knees hitting the float
- Kick with floppy feet

Technical Focus

- Kick comes from the hips
- Legs kick without touching the float
- Kick breaks the water surface
- Hips and tummy up near the surface
- Toes are pointed and ankles relaxed

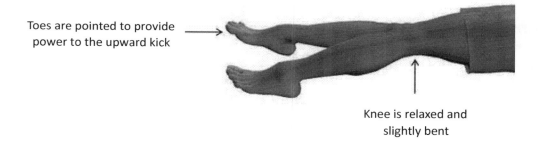

Toes are pointed to provide power to the upward kick

Knee is relaxed and slightly bent

Common Faults

- Kick comes from the knee
- Knees bend and hit the float
- Leg kick is too deep
- Float is held up above the water surface

BACKSTROKE: Legs

Float held overhead with arms straight

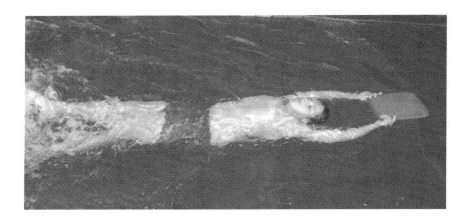

Aim: to enhance a correct body position whilst kicking.

This exercise is a progression from previous leg kick exercises and helps to develop a stronger leg kick.

Key Actions

- Push your hips and chest up to the surface
- Point your toes like a ballerina
- Make your whole body long and straight
- Kick from your hips
- Stretch out and kick hard

Technical Focus

- Kick comes from the hips

- Arms remain either side of the head

- Kick breaks the water surface

- Hips and tummy up near the surface

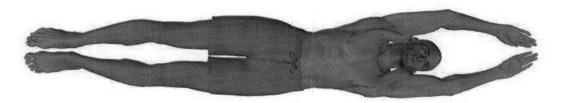

Legs kick and correct body position is maintained throughout.
Note: advanced alternative is shown without holding a float

Common Faults

- Head is raised causing hips and legs to sink

- Hips sink and legs kick too deep

- Toes are turned up

- Head is too far back and the upper body sinks

BACKSTROKE: Legs

Kicking with arms by the sides, hands sculling

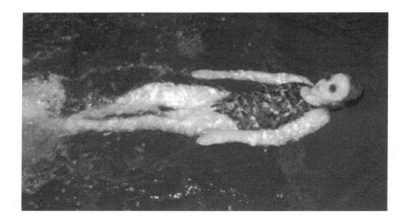

Aim: to practise kicking and maintaining correct body position.

The sculling hand action provides balance and enhances confidence.

Key Actions

- Relax
- Push your hips and chest up to the surface
- Point your toes like a ballerina
- Kick with floppy feet
- Look up to the sky

Technical Focus

- Kick comes from the hips

- Kick is alternating and continuous

- Kick breaks the water surface

- Hips and tummy up near the surface

- Ankles are relaxed and toes are pointed

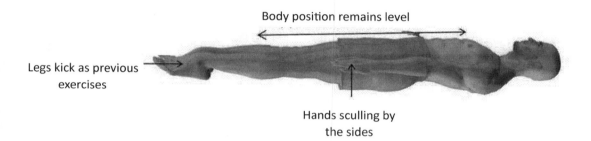

Body position remains level

Legs kick as previous
exercises

Hands sculling by
the sides

Common Faults

- Kick comes from the knee

- Hips sink and legs kick too deep

- Head is too far back

- Body is not relaxed

BACKSTROKE: Arms

Static practice standing on the poolside

Aim: to practise the arm action in its most basic form.

Standing on the poolside allows the swimmer to develop basic technique in a static position.

Key Actions

- Arms brush past your ear
- Fingers closed together
- Arms are continuous
- Stretch your arm all the way up to your ear
- Pull down to your side

Technical Focus

- Arm action is continuous
- Arms stretch all the way up and brush past the ear
- Arms pull down to the side, towards the hip

Arm rises upwards, little finger leading and arm brushing the ear

Hand pulls downwards towards the hip

Common Faults

- Arms are not rising to touch the ear
- Arms are not pulling down to the side
- Pausing in-between arm pulls
- Arms are bending over the head

BACKSTROKE: Arms

Single arm pull with a float held on the chest

Aim: to develop correct arm action whilst kicking.

The float held on the chest provides support for the beginner and the single arm action allows easy learning without compromising the swimmer's coordination.

Key Actions

- Arm brushes past your ear
- Pull down to your thigh
- Fingers closed together
- Little finger enters the water first

Technical Focus

- Arm action is continuous
- Arms stretch all the way up and brush past the ear
- Arms pull down to the thigh
- Fingers are together
- Little finger enters water first

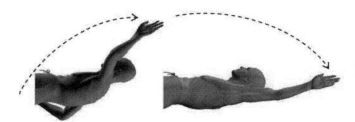 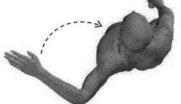

Arm exists the water and brushes past the ear, entering the water little finger first

Arm is bent as it pulls through and straightens as it pull to the thigh

Common Faults

- Arms are pulling out too wide, not brushing the ear
- Arms are not pulling down to the side
- Arms pull too deep under the water
- Fingers are apart
- Thumb enters the water first

BACKSTROKE: Arms

Single arm pull using the lane rope

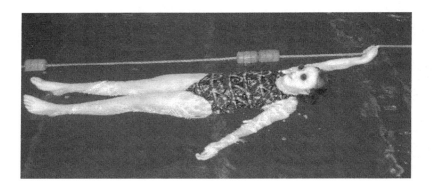

Aim: to develop a bent arm pull using the lane rope to move though the water.

The hand remains fixed on the lane rope as the body is pulled along in the line of the rope. This simulates the bent arm pull action.

Key Actions

- Use the rope to pull you along
- Arms brush past your ear
- Stretch over and hold the rope behind
- Pull fast down the rope
- Thumb comes out first
- Little finger enters the water first

Technical Focus

- Arm action is continuous
- Arms stretch all the way up and brush past the ear
- Arms pull down to the thigh
- Arm action is continuous
- Thumb comes out first

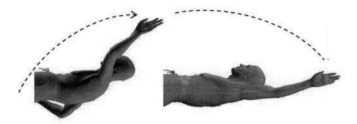 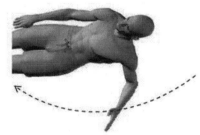

Arm exists the water and brushes past the ear, entering the water little finger first, taking hold of the lane rope

Swimmer pulls from above the head and then pushes past the hips to simulate the bent arm pull action

Common Faults

- Arms are not pulling down to the side
- Elbow is not bending enough
- Arms are bending over the head
- Thumb enters the water first

BACKSTROKE: Arms

Single arm pull with the opposite arm held by the side

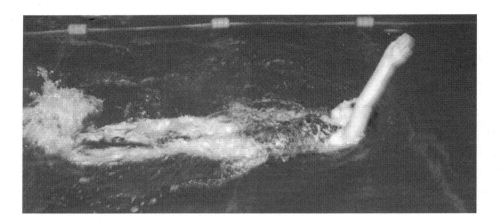

Aim: to practise correct arm action without the aid of floats.

This single arm exercise allows focus on one arm whilst the arm held by the side encourages correct body position.

Key Actions

- Arms brush past your ear
- Arms are continuous
- Pull down to your side
- Pull fast through the water
- Little finger enters the water first

Technical Focus

- Arm action is continuous
- Arms stretch all the way up and brush past the ear
- Arms pull down to the thigh
- Shoulders rock with each arm pull
- Little finger enters the water first

Arm rises upwards, little finger leading and arm brushing the ear

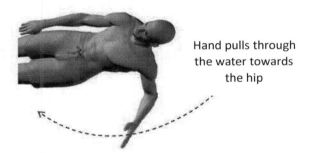

Hand pulls through the water towards the hip

Common Faults

- Arms are pulling out too wide, not brushing the ear
- Arms are not pulling down to the side
- Arms pull too deep under the water
- Arms are bending over the head

BACKSTROKE: Arms

Arms only with pull-buoy held between legs

Aim: to develop a continual arm action using both arms.

The pull-buoy provides support and helps to isolate the arms by preventing the leg kick action. Note: it is normal for the legs to 'sway' from side to side during this exercise.

Key Actions

- Arms brush past your ear
- Fingers closed together
- Continuous arm action
- Pull hard through the water and down to your side
- Allow your legs to 'sway' side to side

Technical Focus

- Arm action is continuous and steady

- Arms stretch all the way over and brush past the ear

- Arms pull down to the thigh

- Shoulders rock evenly side to side

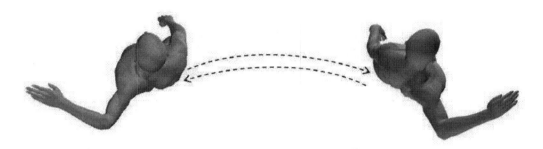

Continual arm action causes an even rocking of the shoulders

Common Faults

- Pause between arm pulls

- Arms are pulling out too wide, not brushing the ear

- Arms are not pulling down to the side

- Arms pull too deep under the water

BACKSTROKE: Breathing

Full stroke with breathing

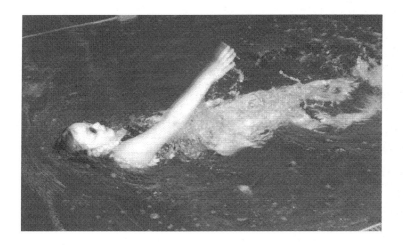

Aim: to focus on breathing in time with the stroke actions.

The swimmer should breathe in and out in regular rhythm with the arm action. This exercise can be incorporated into any of the previous arm action exercises, depending on the ability of the swimmer.

Key Actions

• Breathe in time with your arms

• Breathe in with one arm pull and out with the other

Technical Focus

• Breathing should be regular and rhythmical

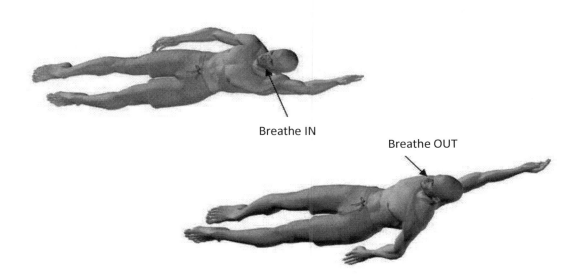

Breathe IN

Breathe OUT

Common Faults

• Holding the breath
• Breathing too rapidly

BACKSTROKE: Timing

Push and glide adding arms and legs

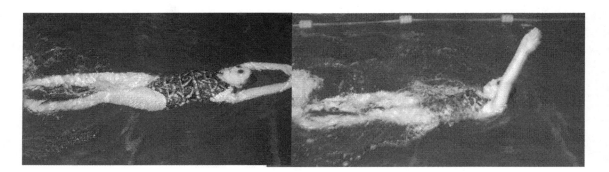

Aim: to practise and develop coordination and stroke timing.

The swimmer performs a push and glide to establish correct body position, then adds arm and leg actions.

Key Points

• Count in your head to 3 with each arm pull

• Kick 3 times with each arm pull

• Keep the arm pull continuous

• Keep the leg kick continuous

Technical Focus

- 3 leg kicks per arm pull
- Leg kick should be continuous
- Arm action should be regular

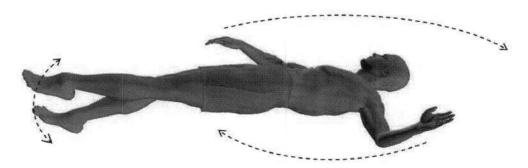

One arm exits the water as the other begins to pull and the leg kick remains continuous

Common Faults

- One leg kick per arm pull ('one beat cycle')
- Continuous leg kick but not enough arm pulls
- Arm pull is too irregular
- Stroke cycle is not regular and continuous

BACKSTROKE

Full stroke

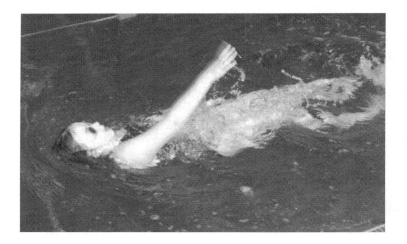

Aim: to demonstrate full stroke backstroke showing continuous and alternating arm and leg actions, with correct timing, resulting in a smooth and efficient stroke.

Key Actions

- Kick from your hips

- Relax

- Keep your hips and tummy at the surface

- Make a small splash with your toes

- Continuous arm action

- Arms brush past your ear and pull to your side

Technical Focus

- Body position should be horizontal and flat
- Leg kick should be continuous and alternating
- Arm action is continuous
- Leg kick breaks the water surface
- 3 legs kicks per arm pull

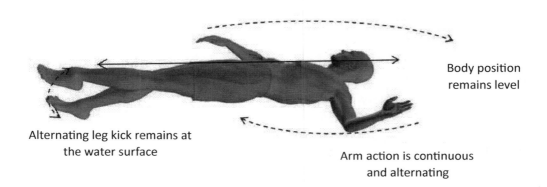

Body position remains level

Alternating leg kick remains at the water surface

Arm action is continuous and alternating

Common Faults

- Hips and abdomen sink
- Legs kick too deep or weak
- Arms pull one at a time
- Arms pull too wide or too deep

Real Backstroke Questions

Problems and difficulties come from the fact that swimming on your back means you cannot see where you are going! Sounds obvious but when we swim in a prone position (on our front facing forwards) we can see around us and therefore are totally aware of our surroundings. When swimming along whilst facing the sky we lose most of our surrounding awareness.

Without knowing we then lift our head slightly and this instantly causes the hips to drop and the legs and the rest of the body then follow on. The result: that sinking feeling.

"How do I prevent myself from sinking?"

Mark's answer:

"When swimming backstroke ensure your head is back enough that your ears are submerged. Then stretch out so that your hips, legs and feet come to the surface. Your leg kick should break the water surface enough to produce a small splash.

Do not fall into the trap of trying to look for your feet or at your flat body position. Moving your head only the slightest inch to check will instantly result in that sinking feeling again. If you can feel your toes breaking the water surface then the chances are your body position is somewhere near correct."

"How do I relax on my back and why do I not float when swimming backstroke?"

Mark's answer:

"Floating is a characteristic of the human body. Some of us float well and some of us simply do not. It is all down to relative density. Basically fat floats and muscle sinks, which is why lean or muscular people tend to sink.

Focus on your backstroke swimming technique and then remaining in the correct position at the water surface will take care of itself.

Become more relaxed in a supine position (on your back) in the water by floating in a star position, with arms and legs wide. This wide body position helps you to remain afloat and therefore relax. Even if you are a poor floater, the ability to relax will help all aspect of your swimming."

Chapter 15: Breaststroke

Basic Breaststroke Technique

Breaststroke is the oldest and slowest of the four swimming strokes. It is also the most inefficient of all strokes, which is what makes it the slowest. Propulsion from the arms and legs is a consecutive action that takes place under the water. A large frontal resistance area is created as the heels draw up towards the seat and the breathing technique inclines the body position also increasing resistance. These are the main reasons that make breaststroke inefficient and slow.

This stroke is normally one of the first strokes to be taught, especially to adults, as the head and face is clear of the water, giving the swimmer a greater perception of their whereabouts and their buoyancy. There are variations in the overall technique, ranging from a slow recreational style to a more precise competitive style. Body position should be as flat and streamlined as possible with an inclination from the head to the feet so that the leg kick recovery takes place under the water.

The leg kick as a whole should be a simultaneous and flowing action, providing the majority of the propulsion.

The arm action should also be simultaneous and flowing and overall provides the smallest propulsive phase of the four strokes.

The stroke action gives a natural body lift, which gives the ideal breathing point with each stroke. A streamlined body position during the timing sequence of the arm and leg action is essential to capitalise on the propulsive phases of the stroke.

Body Position

The body position should be inclined slightly downwards from the head to the feet.

The body should be as flat and streamlined as possible with an inclination from the head to the feet so that the leg kick recovery takes place under the water.

Head movement should be kept to a minimum and the shoulders should remain level throughout the stroke.

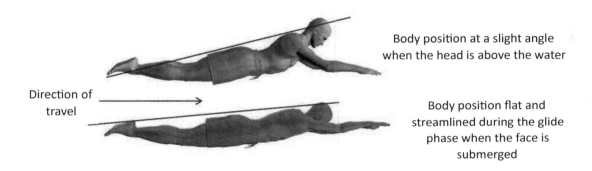

Body position at a slight angle when the head is above the water

Direction of travel

Body position flat and streamlined during the glide phase when the face is submerged

The main aim should be good streamlining, however the underwater recovery movements of the arms and legs together with the lifting of the head to breathe, all compromise the overall body position. In order to reduce resistance created by these movements, as the propulsive phase of an arm pull or leg kick takes place, the opposite end of the body remains still and streamlined.

Common Body Position Mistakes

The most common mistake with the body position for breaststroke is being too flat in the water. In other words the face is submerged too much causing the hips, legs and feet to rise to the surface. This could then make lifting the face to the front to breathe more difficult. It could also lead to the feet breaking the surface of the water as they kick and therefore losing power.

The angled body position can be perfected with a simple push and glide exercise. Push and glide from the poolside either holding a float or without, but with the head and face up above the water surface.

Leg Kick

The most important teaching aspect of the legs is that the action is a series of movements that flow together to make one sweeping leg kicking action.

 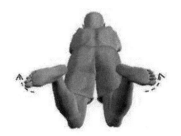 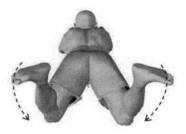

| Heels are drawn up towards the seat, soles face upwards | Feet turn outwards to allow the heels and soles to aid propulsion | Heels push back and outwards in a whip-like action |

It is more important for a swimmer or teacher to recognise the difference between the wedge kick and the whip kick in breaststroke. The leg action provides the largest amount of propulsion in the stroke and swimmers will favour a wedge kick or a whip kick depending on which comes most naturally. For a whip kick, the legs kick in a whip-like action with the knees remaining close together. For a wedge kick the legs kick in a wider, more deliberate circular path.

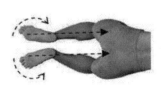  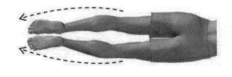

| Heels drawn towards the seat and feet turn outwards | Heels drive back in a circular whip-like action giving the kick power and motion | Kick finishes in a streamlined position with legs straight and toes pointed |

The leg kick as a whole should be a simultaneous and flowing action, providing the majority of the propulsion. Knees bend as the heels are drawn up towards the seat and toes are turned out ready for the heels and soles of the feet to drive the water backwards. The legs sweep outwards and downwards in a flowing circular path, accelerating as they kick and return together and straight, providing a streamlined position.

Common Leg Kick Mistakes

The feet cause most of the problems when it comes to kicking. Failure to turn the feet out will result in a lack of power and that feeling of going nowhere. Failure to turn out both feet and only turning out one foot will result in something known as a screw kick. This is where one leg kicks correctly and the other swings around providing no propulsion at all.

The best exercise for correcting these common faults is to swim on your back (supine) with a woggle or noodle held under the arms for support. Then the swimmer is able to sit up slightly and watch their own leg kick as they perform it. Kicking in slow motion at first making a conscious effort to turn out both feet and ensure both legs and feet are symmetrical is best before attempting to add power.

Arm Action

The amount of propulsion generated from arm technique has developed over the years as the stroke has changed to become more competitive. The arm action overall provides the smallest propulsive phase of the four competitive strokes.

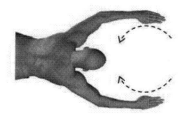

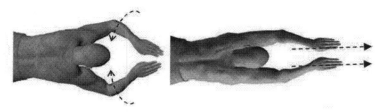

Elbows tuck in and arms and hands stretch forward into a glide

Arms and hands pull around and downwards

Catch

The arm action begins with the arms fully extended out in front, fingers and hands together. The hands pitch outwards and downwards to an angle of about 45 degrees at the start of the catch phase. The arms pull outwards and downwards until they are approximately shoulder width apart. Elbows begin to bend and shoulders roll inwards at the end of the catch phase.

Propulsive Phase

The arms sweep downwards and inwards and the hands pull to their deepest point. Elbows bend to 90 degrees and remain high. At the end of the down sweep, the hands sweep inwards and slightly upwards. Elbows tuck into the sides as the hands are pulled inwards towards the chest and the chin.

Recovery

The hands recover by stretching forwards in a streamlined position. Hands recover under, on or over the water surface, depending on the style of stroke to be taught.

Common arm pull mistakes

The arm technique for this stroke usually becomes the dominant force when it should not. It is very common for swimmers to put more effort into pulling themselves through the water, when it should be the leg kick providing the power and momentum.

In an attempt to haul them through the water the arm pull is too big and too wide. It is not uncommon to pull arms completely to the side, making for an inefficient recovery under the water surface, which will almost certainly result in the swimmer slowing down.

An easy exercise to practice to help perfect the arm pull technique is to walk slowly through shallow water of about shoulder depth, ensuring the arms pull in small circles and the hands remain in front of the swimmer at all times. They should also extend forwards and remain there momentarily for the glide phase.

Breathing

Breaststroke has a natural body lift during the stroke, which gives the ideal breathing point during each stroke cycle.

Inhalation takes place at the end of the arm in sweep as the body allows the head to lift clear of the water. The head should be lifted enough for the mouth to clear the surface and inhale, but not excessively so as to keep the frontal resistance created by this movement to a minimum.

Breathe IN

Inhalation occurs as the arms pull down and the head rises above the surface

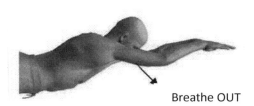

Breathe OUT

Exhalation occurs as the arms recover out in front

Explosive or trickle breathing can be utilised.

The head returns to the water to exhale as the arms stretch forward to begin their recovery phase.

Some swimmers perform the stroke with the head raised throughout to keep the mouth and nose clear of the water at all times. This simplifies the breathing but at the expense of a greater frontal resistance.

Common Breathing Mistakes

Some beginners experience difficulty breathing during breaststroke. The two main reasons are failing to lift the head enough to clear the water surface and breathe, and holding the breath and therefore failing to breathe out into the water.

Breaststroke needs a powerful leg kick and it is this leg kick that gives a natural body lift. Together with the arm action there should be enough lift to enable the mouth to clear the water surface for inhalation to take place.

The most common mistake made with breaststroke breathing is failing to exhale during the glide phase making it impossible to inhale again, or forcing the swimmer to use an explosive breathing technique.

Although explosive breathing is a valid breathing technique for this swimming stroke, it is usually only used competitively.

When swum recreationally, exhaling during the glide phase of the stroke is more efficient and uses less energy.

Using a woggle under the arms provides support and allows the swimmer to swim in slow motion whilst practicing the breathing technique. Extending the body into a long glide as exhalation takes place ensures the breathing occurs at the correct time and keeps the stroke at its most efficient.

Timing and Coordination

The coordination of the propulsive phases should be a continuous alternating action, where one propulsive phase takes over as one ends. The stroke timing can be summed up with the following sequence: pull, breathe, kick, glide.

A streamlined body position at the end of that sequence is essential to capitalise on the propulsive phases of the stroke. The timing can be considered in another way: when the arms are pulling in their propulsive phase, the legs are streamlined and when the legs are kicking in propulsion, the arms are streamlined.

| Body position starts with hands and feet together | Pull, breathe, kick, glide sequence is performed | Swimmer returns to the original position |

Full body extension is essential before the start of each stroke cycle.

Decreasing or even eliminating the glide and using the arm and leg actions in an almost continuous stroke to give more propulsion are a more competitive variation of stroke timing.

Common Timing Mistakes

As this stoke is a simultaneous stroke it is very common to kick with the legs and pull with the arms at the same time. The result will be a very inefficient swimming stroke as the arms and legs counter act each other.

To ensure the timing and coordination of the arms and legs are correct the swimmer must focus on performing an arm pull followed by a leg kick, or on 'kicking their hands forwards'. In other words as their legs kick round and back, their arms must extend forwards. This ensures that the arms and legs are working efficiently and are extended out together during the glide phase.

Full Stroke Overview

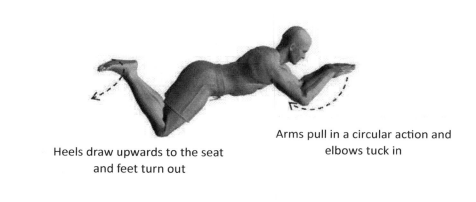

Heels draw upwards to the seat
and feet turn out

Arms pull in a circular action and
elbows tuck in

Legs kick backwards
providing power and
propulsion

Arms stretch forwards
into a glide

Breaststroke Exercises

The next section contains practical exercises to help learn and fine-tune each separate part of your breaststroke technique.

They are designed to isolate each element of the stroke so that you can learn exactly what each part of your body should be doing.

BREASTSTROKE: Body Position

Push and glide

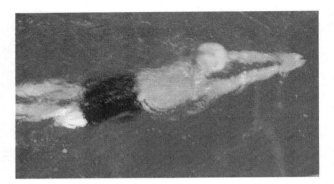

Aim: to develop a basic body position by pushing from the side.

The distance of the glide will be limited due to the resistance created by the chest and shoulders. The exercise can be performed with the face submerged as it would be during the glide phase of the stroke or with the head up facing forwards.

Key Actions

- Push hard from the side
- Keep head up looking forward
- Stretch out as far as you can
- Keep your hands together
- Keep your feet together

Technical Focus

- Head remains still and central

- Face is up so that only the chin is in the water

- Eyes are looking forwards over the surface

- Shoulders should be level and square

- Hips are slightly below shoulder level

- Legs are in line with the body

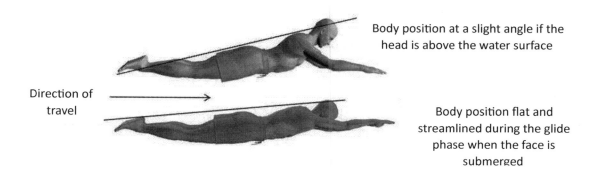

Body position at a slight angle if the head is above the water surface

Direction of travel

Body position flat and streamlined during the glide phase when the face is submerged

Common Faults

- Shoulders and/or hips are not level

- Head is not central and still

- One shoulder is in front of the other

BREASTSTROKE: Legs

Sitting on the poolside with feet in the water

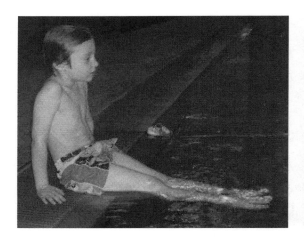 

Aim: to practice the leg action whilst sat stationary on the poolside.

This exercise allows the pupil to copy the teacher who can also be sat on the poolside demonstrating the leg kick. The physical movement can be learnt before attempting the leg kick in the water.

Key Actions

- Kick your legs simultaneously
- Keep your knees close together
- Kick like a frog
- Make sure your legs are straight and together at the end of the kick

Technical Focus

- Kick should be simultaneous

- Legs should be a mirror image

- Heels are drawn towards the seat

- The feet turn out just before the kick

- Feet come together at the end of the kick with legs straight and toes pointed

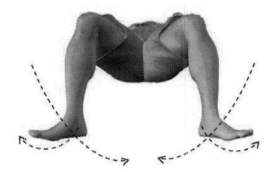

Feet turn out as the legs begin to kick around in a circular motion

Common Faults

- Circular kick in the opposite direction

- Only turning one foot out

- Legs are not straight at the end of the kick

- Leg action is not circular

BREASTSTROKE: Legs

Supine position with a woggle held under the arms

Aim: to develop breaststroke leg kick in a supine position.

This allows the swimmer to see their legs kicking. The woggle provides stability for the beginner and, with the swimmer in a supine position, allows the teacher easy communication during the exercise.

Key Actions

- Kick with both legs at the same time

- Keep your feet in the water

- Kick like a frog

- Kick and glide

- Point your toes at the end of the kick

Technical Focus

- Kick should be simultaneous
- Heels are drawn towards the seat
- The feet turn out just before the kick
- Feet kick back with knees just inline with the hips
- Feet come together at the end of the kick

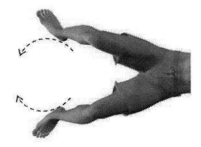

Heels drive back in a circular whip-like action
giving the kick power and motion

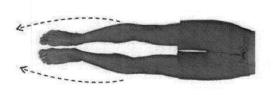

Kick finishes in a streamlined position with legs
straight and toes pointed

Common Faults

- Feet are coming out of the water
- Failing to bring the heels up to the bottom
- Leg kick is not simultaneous
- Legs are not straight at the end of the kick

201

BREASTSTROKE: Legs

Static practice holding the poolside

Aim: to practise breaststroke leg action in a static position.

This allows the swimmer to develop correct technique in a prone position in the water. Kicking WITHOUT force and power should be encouraged during this exercise to avoid undue impact on the lower back.

Key Actions

- Kick both legs at the same time
- Kick like a frog
- Draw a circle with your heels
- Make sure your legs are straight at the end of the kick

Technical Focus

- Legs should be a mirror image
- Heels are drawn towards the seat
- The feet turn out just before the kick
- Feet kick back with knees inline with the hips
- Feet come together at the end of the kick with legs straight and toes pointed

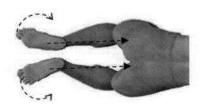

Heels drawn towards the seat as the feet turn out

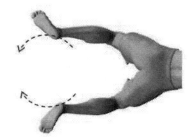

Heels kick around in a circular motion

Common Faults

- Only turning one foot out
- Legs are not simultaneous
- Leg action is not circular

BREASTSTROKE: Legs

Prone position with a float held under each arm

Aim: to practise and develop correct leg technique in a prone position.

Using two floats aids balance and stability and encourages correct body position whilst moving through the water.

Key Actions

- Keep your knees close together
- Point your toes to your shins
- Drive the water backwards with your heels
- Glide with legs straight at the end of the each kick

Technical Focus

- Leg kick should be simultaneous
- Heels are drawn towards the seat
- The feet turn out just before the kick
- Feet kick back with knees inline with the hips
- Feet come together at the end of the kick

 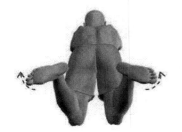 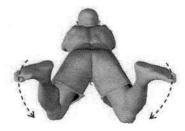

Heels are drawn up towards the seat, soles face upwards	Feet turn outwards to allow the heels and soles to aid propulsion	Heels push back and outwards in a whip-like action

Common Faults

- One foot turns out, causing a 'scissor' like kick
- Legs kick back and forth
- Legs kick is not simultaneous
- Toes are not pointed at the end of the kick

BREASTSTROKE: Legs

Holding a float out in front with both hands

Aim: to practise and learn correct kicking technique and develop leg strength.

Holding a single float or kickboard out in front isolates the legs and creates a slight resistance which demands a stronger kick with which to maintain momentum.

Key Actions

- Drive the water backwards with force
- Turn your feet out and drive the water with your heels
- Kick and glide
- Kick like a frog
- Make your feet like a penguin

Technical Focus

- Kick should be simultaneous

- Legs drive back to provide momentum

- Heels are drawn towards the seat

- The feet turn out before the kick

- Feet come together at the end of the kick with legs straight and toes pointed

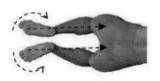  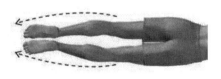

| Heels drawn towards the seat and feet turn outwards | Heels drive back in a circular whip-like action giving the kick power and motion | Kick finishes in a streamlined position with legs straight and toes pointed |

Common Faults

- Kick is slow and lacking power

- Failing to bring the heels up to the bottom

- Feet are breaking the water surface

- Toes are not pointed at the end of the kick

BREASTSTROKE: Legs

Arms stretched out in front holding a float vertically

Aim: to develop leg kick strength and power.

The float held vertically adds resistance to the movement and requires the swimmer to kick with greater effort. This exercise is ideal for strengthening with a weak leg kick.

Key Actions

- Kick your legs simultaneously
- Push the water with your heels and the soles of your feet
- Drive the water backwards with your heels

Technical Focus

- Arms should be straight and float should be held partly underwater
- Kick should be a whip like action
- Feet kick back with knees inline with the hips
- Feet come together at the end of the kick

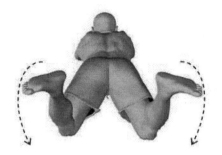 

Heels push back and outwards in a
whip-like action

Heels drive back to add power to the kick

Common Faults

- Float is held flat or out of the water
- Not turning both feet out
- Leg kick lacks sufficient power

BREASTSTROKE: Legs

Supine position with hands held on hips

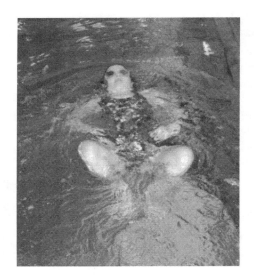

Aim: to develop leg kick strength and stamina.

This exercise is more advanced and requires the leg kick to be previously well practised.

Key Actions

- Keep your feet in the water
- Kick like a frog
- Make sure your legs are straight after each kick
- Kick and glide
- Point your toes at the end of the kick

Technical Focus

- Kick should be simultaneous

- Heels are drawn towards the seat

- The feet turn out just before the kick

- Feet kick back with knees inline with the hips

- Feet come together at the end of the kick with legs straight and toes pointed

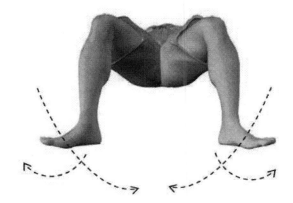

Feet turn out as the legs begin to kick around in a circular action

Common Faults

- Not turning both feet out

- Kick is not hard enough to provide power

- Legs are not straight at the end of the kick

- Toes are not pointed at the end of the kick

BREASTSTROKE: Legs

Moving practice with arms stretched out in front

Aim: to practise correct kicking technique and develop leg strength.

This is an advanced exercise as holding the arms out in front demands a stronger kick with which to maintain momentum whilst maintaining a streamlined body position.

Key Actions

- Keep your knees close together
- Drive the water with your heels
- Make sure your legs are straight at the end of the kick
- Kick and glide

Technical Focus

- Kick should be simultaneous

- The feet turn out just before the kick

- Feet kick back with knees just inline with the hips

- Feet come together at the end of the kick with legs straight and toes pointed

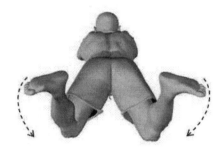

Heels push back and outwards in a
whip-like action

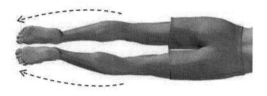

Kick finishes in a streamlined position
with legs straight and toes pointed

Common Faults

- Not turning both feet out

- Feet are breaking the water surface

- Legs are not straight at the end of the kick

- Toes are not pointed at the end of the kick

BREASTSTROKE: Arms

Static practice standing on the poolside

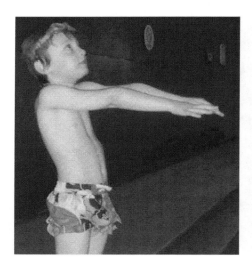 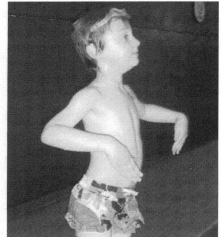

Aim: to learn the arm pull technique in its most basic form.

On the poolside, either sitting or standing, the swimmer can practise and perfect the movement without the resistance of the water.

Key Actions

- Both arms pull at the same time
- Keep your fingers closed together
- Keep your hands flat
- Tuck your elbows into your sides after each pull
- Stretch your arms forward until they are straight
- Draw an upside down heart with your hands

Technical Focus

- Arm action should be simultaneous

- Fingers should be together

- Arm pull should be circular

- Elbows should be tucked in after each pull

- Arms should extend forward and together after each pull

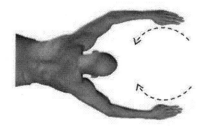

Arms and hands pull around and downwards

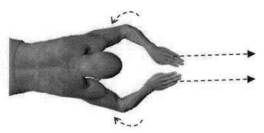

Elbows tuck in and arms extend forward

Common Faults

- Fingers apart

- Arms pull at different speeds

- Arms pull past the shoulders

- Elbows fail to tuck in each time

- Arms fail to extend full forward

BREASTSTROKE: Arms

Walking practice moving through shallow water

 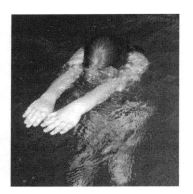

Aim: to practise and develop correct arm technique from in the water.

The swimmer can experience the feel of pulling the water whilst walking along the pool floor. Where the water is too deep, this exercise can be performed standing on the poolside. Submerging the face is optional at this stage.

Key Actions

- Pull with both arms at the same time
- Keep your hands under the water
- Tuck your elbows into your sides after each pull
- Stretch your arms forward until they are straight
- Draw an upside down heart with your hands

Technical Focus

- Arm action should be simultaneous
- Arms and hands should remain under water
- Fingers should be together
- Arms should extend forward and together until straight after each pull

Arms and hands pull back in
a circular motion

Elbows tuck in and arms and hands stretch
forwards into a glide

Common Faults

- Fingers are apart
- Arms pull past the shoulders
- Elbows fail to tuck in each time
- Arms fail to extend full forward
- Hands come out of the water

BREASTSTROKE: Arms

Moving practice with a woggle held under the arms

Aim: to learn correct arm action whilst moving through the water.

The use of the woggle means that leg kicks are not required to assist motion and this then helps develop strength in the arm pull. The woggle slightly restricts arm action but not enough to negate the benefits of this exercise.

Key Actions

- Pull round in a circle
- Keep your hands under the water
- Keep your fingers together and hands flat
- Pull your body through the water
- Draw an upside down heart with your hands

Technical Focus

- Arm action should be simultaneous

- Arms and hands should remain under water

- Arms and hands should extend forward after the pull

- Fingers should be together

- Arm pull should be circular

Arms and hands pull around
and downwards

Elbows tuck in and arms and hands stretch
forwards into a glide

Common Faults

- Fingers are apart

- Arms fail to extend fully forward

- Hands come out of the water

- Arms extend forward too far apart

BREASTSTROKE: Arms

Arms only with a pull-buoy held between the legs

Aim: to develop strength in the arm pull.

The pull-buoy prevents the legs from kicking, therefore isolating the arms. As the legs are stationary, forward propulsion and a glide action is difficult and therefore the arm action is made stronger as it has to provide all the propulsion for this exercise.

Key Actions

- Keep your hands under the water
- Pull your body through the water
- Keep your elbows high as you pull
- Tuck your elbows into your sides after each pull
- Stretch your arms forward until they are straight

Technical Focus

- Arms and hands should remain under water
- Arm pull should be circular
- Elbows should be tucked in after each pull
- Arms should extend forward and together

Arms and hands pull back in a
circular motion

Elbows tuck in and arms and hands
stretch forwards together

Common Faults

- Arms pull past the shoulders
- Elbows fail to tuck in each time
- Arms fail to extend full forward
- Hands come out of the water
- Arms extend forward too far apart

BREASTSTROKE: Arms

Push and glide adding arm pulls

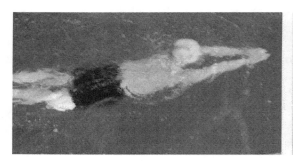 

Aim: to progress arm action and technique from previous exercises.

By incorporating a push and glide, this allows the swimmer to practise maintaining a correct body position whilst using the arms. This is a more advanced exercise as the number of arms pulls and distance travelled will vary according to the strength of the swimmer.

Key Actions

- Keep your hands under the water
- Pull your body through the water
- Tuck your elbows into your sides after each pull
- Stretch your arms forward with hands together

Technical Focus

- Arms and hands should remain under water
- Elbows should be tucked in after each pull
- Arms should extend forward into a glide position
- Body position should be maintained throughout

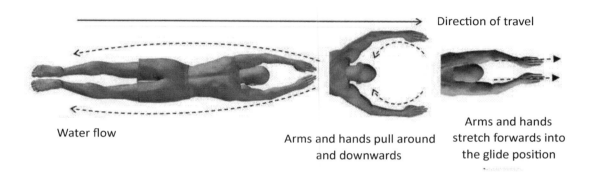

Direction of travel

Water flow

Arms and hands pull around and downwards

Arms and hands stretch forwards into the glide position

Common Faults

- Arms pull past the shoulders
- Arms fail to extend full forward
- Hands come out of the water
- Arms extend forward too far apart
- Arms fail to bend during the pull

BREASTSTROKE: Breathing

Static practice, breathing with arm action

Aim: to practise breaststroke breathing action whilst standing in the water.

This allows the swimmer to experience the feel of breathing into the water in time with the arm action, without the need to actually swim.

Key Actions

- Breathe in as you complete your arm pull
- Breathe out as your hands stretch forwards
- Blow your hands forwards

Technical Focus

- Breath inwards at the end of the in sweep
- Head lifts up as the arms complete the pull
- Head should clear the water
- Head returns to the water as the arms recover
- Breath out is as the hands recover forward

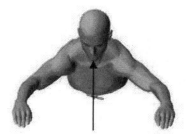

Breathe IN as the arms pull
down and the head rises

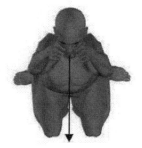

Breathe OUT as the arms recover
forwards and the face enters the
water

Common Faults

- Head fails to clear the water
- Breathing out as the arms pull back
- Lifting the head to breathe as the arms recover

BREASTSTROKE: Breathing

Breathing practice with woggle under the arms

Aim: to develop correct synchronisation of breathing and arm pull technique.

The woggle provides support, which enables the exercise to be done slowly at first. It also allows the swimmer to travel during the practice. Leg action can be added if necessary. Note: the woggle can restrict complete arm action.

Key Actions

- Breathe in as you complete your arm pull
- Breathe out as your hands stretch forwards
- Blow your hands forwards

Technical Focus

- Breath inwards at the end of the in-sweep
- Head lifts up as the arms complete the pull back
- Head should clear the water
- Head returns to the water as the arms recover
- Breathing out is as the hands stretch forward

Breathe IN

Breathing in occurs as the arms pull down and
the head rises above the surface

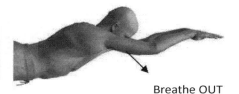

Breathe OUT

Breathing out occurs as the arms recover and
stretch forwards

Common Faults

- Holding the breath
- Head fails to clear the water
- Breathing out as the arms pull back
- Lifting the head as the arms stretch forward

BREASTSTROKE: Breathing

Float held in front, breathing with leg kick

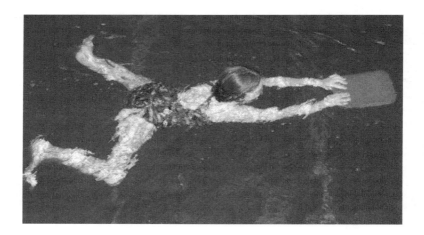

Aim: to develop the breathing technique in time with the leg kick.

The float provides stability and allows the swimmer to focus on the breathe, kick, glide sequence.

Key Actions

- Breathe in as your legs bend ready to kick
- Breathe out as you kick and glide
- Kick your head down

Technical Focus

- Inward breathing should be just before the knees bend
- Head lifts up as the knees bend ready to kick
- Mouth should clear the water
- Head returns to the water as the legs thrust backwards
- Breathe out is as the legs kick into a glide

Breathe IN just before the knees bend for the kick

Breathe OUT as the legs kick into a glide

Common Faults

- Holding the breath
- Head fails to clear the water
- Breathing out as the knees bend ready to kick
- Lifting the head as the legs kick into a glide

BREASTSTROKE: Timing

Slow practice with woggle under the arms

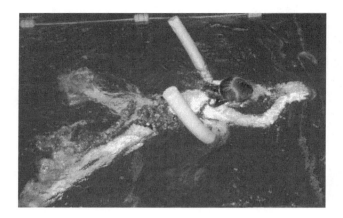

Aim: to practise the stroke timing in its most basic form.

The use of the woggle placed under the arms allows the swimmer to practice the exercise in stages as slowly as they need. It must be noted that the woggle resists against the glide and therefore the emphasis must be placed on the timing of the arms and legs. The glide can be developed using other exercises.

Key Actions

- Pull with your hands first
- Kick your hands forwards
- Kick your body into a glide
- Pull, breathe, kick, glide

Technical Focus

- From a streamlined position arms should pull first
- Legs should kick into a glide
- Legs should kick as the hands and arms recover
- A glide should precede the next arm pull

| Body position starts with hands and feet together | Pull, breathe, kick, glide sequence is performed | Swimmer returns to starting body position |

Common Faults

- Kicking and pulling at the same time
- Failure to glide
- Legs kick whilst gliding

BREASTSTROKE: Timing

Push and glide, adding stroke cycles

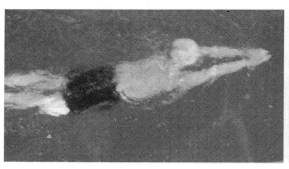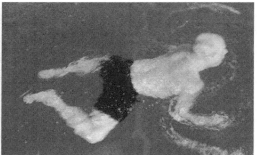

Aim: to practise and develop correct stroke timing.

The swimmer starts with a push and glide to establish a streamlined glide. The arm pull, breath in and then leg kick is executed in the correct sequence, resulting in another streamlined glide.

Key Actions

- Kick your hands forwards
- Kick your body into a glide
- Pull, breathe, kick, glide

Technical Focus

- From a streamlined position arms should pull first
- Legs should kick into a glide
- Legs should kick as the hands and arms recover
- A glide should precede the next arm pull

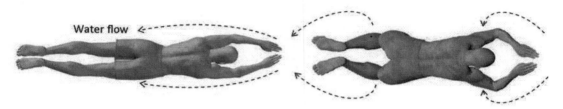

Push and glide to establish body position   Pull, breathe, kick and glide again

Common Faults

- Kicking and pulling at the same time
- Failure to glide
- Legs kick whilst gliding

BREASTSTROKE: Timing

Two kicks, one arm pull

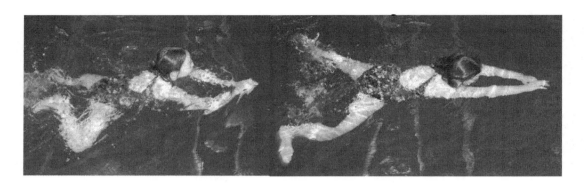

Aim: to perfect timing whilst maintaining a streamlined body position.

From a push and glide, the swimmer performs a 'pull, breathe, kick, glide' stroke cycle into another streamlined glide. They then perform an additional kick whilst keeping the hands and arms stretched out in front. This encourages concentration on timing and coordination and at the same time develops leg kick strength.

Key Actions

- Kick your body into a glide
- Pull, breathe, kick, glide

Technical Focus

- Legs should kick into a glide
- Legs should kick as the hands and arms recover
- A glide should follow each leg kick
- Head lifts to breath with each arm pull

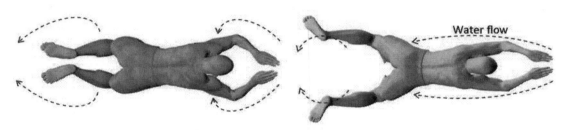

A full stroke cycle is performed
from a push and glide

Additional kick whilst the hands and
arms remain stretched out in front

Common Faults

- Arms pull too often and too early
- Failure to glide
- Failure to keep the hands together for the second kick

BREASTSTROKE

Full stroke

Aim: to swim full stroke Breast Stroke demonstrating efficient arm and leg action, with regular breathing and correct timing.

Key Actions

- Kick and glide

- Kick your hands forwards

- Drive your feet backward through the water

- Keep your fingers together and under the water

- Pull in a small circle then stretch forward

- Breath with each stroke

Technical Focus

- Head remains still and central
- Shoulders remain level
- Leg kick is simultaneous
- Feet turn out and drive backwards
- Arm action should be circular and simultaneous
- Breathing is regular with each stroke cycle

| Heels draw up to the seat and feet turn outwards | Arms pull in a circular action and elbows tuck inwards | Legs kick backwards providing power and propulsion | Arms stretch forward into a glide |

Common Faults

- Failure to glide
- Stroke is rushed
- Leg kick is not simultaneous
- Arms pull to the sides
- Failing to breath regularly

Real Breaststroke Questions

"I would like some tips on how to swim breaststroke with more speed. Which parts of my breaststroke technique could I change to gain more speed?"

Mark's answer:

"The propulsion for breaststroke comes from having a powerful leg kick, but speed over a longer distance comes from the glide phase of the stroke.

Firstly develop the power and technique of your leg kick by kicking whilst holing onto a float or kick board. Ensure your leg kick is complete by bringing your feet together and straightening out your legs at the end of each kick phase. Each kick should be a powerful whip action, keeping your knees relatively close together.

The power and strength of your leg kick can be enhanced and improved by holding the float in a vertical position in the water. This will add frontal resistance and make the exercise more intense and therefore will force your legs to have to kick with more power and work harder.

Next ensure that your arms are fully extended at the end of each arm pull phase. The circular motion of the arm action should be a small circle just in front of you. A common mistake is to pull wide and allow the hands to pull past the shoulders. Fully extending the arms and hands after each arm pull will ensure that the maximum distance is covered with each stroke.

Correct timing ensures an effective glide phase. The glide phase occurs just after the legs kick back and round and arms extend forward. Wait momentarily and glide for a second or two with arms together and feet together in a streamlined position in the water.

A good swimming exercise for improving breaststroke timing and body position is to swim using two leg kicks and one arm pull cycles. In other words swim a breaststroke cycle normally (pull, breathe, kick, glide) and then hold the glide position with the arms and add an additional leg kick.

You can experiment with gliding for different lengths of time. The longer the glide, the less strokes it will take to get to the end of the pool, but glide for too long and you will slow down and lose momentum.

Competitive breaststroke contains virtually no glide phase, as the arms pull as soon as the leg kick is complete. The speed of the stroke comes from the power and strength of the arm pull and the leg kick, combined with the arms and legs fully extending to gain as much distance per stroke cycle as possible.

A combination of all of the above tips and exercises will help make your breaststroke faster."

"Will I lose weight swimming breaststroke? I want to start swimming for weight loss and the most enjoyable style for me is the breaststroke. But, I don't like to put my face in the water."

Mark's answer:

"Swimming breaststroke without putting your face in the water is probably one of the most common ways of swimming. The fact that it is technically incorrect is of no importance if that is the way you wish to swim.

If weight loss is your goal then go for it. Swimming is arguably one of the best ways of burning calories, toning your muscles and changing your body shape. But keep one very important thing in mind...

Swimming is easy to take it easy. If you plod up and down the pool at a gentle pace it will not be a challenge to your body. You will then burn very little calories and the result will be little or no weight loss.

So, you absolutely must take yourself out of your comfort zone. In other words get out of breath in the same way you would if you were to do a workout at the gym. To achieve this in the pool simply try swimming one length as fast as you can and then a slower length to recover. Repeat this as many times as you can for at least 20 minutes.

As you become fitter and your weight goes down your swimming will begin to feel easy again, so change the pattern. Maybe do 2 lengths at speed and only one to recover. Maybe take a float and just use your legs to give them a workout. Maybe try one length full speed, one medium pace and then one slow.

There are hundreds of ways of varying your swimming even if you only swim one stroke one way. The point is to keep it challenging for your body and at the same time it remains interesting. Also your weight loss is less likely to plateau and your fitness and body shape will continue to change the way you want it to."

"Why do my legs sink whenever I swim breaststroke? Is it because my kick is not strong enough?"

Mark's answer:

"You could be right in your assumption that your breaststroke leg kick is not strong or powerful enough and therefore is the cause of your legs sinking as you swim.

The power of the kick is vital for maintaining the movement and momentum of the stroke and the majority of the drive of the stroke should come from the leg kick. Correct body position and a smooth glide will also help maintain momentum and reduce or prevent your legs sinking.

Ensure that when you kick, you drive your heels back and around in a whip-like action. The surface area of the underside of each foot and your heel should be facing backwards as if pushing away from the pool wall. That way they can push on the water to provide maximum power.

To help strengthen your leg kick, try kicking whilst holding a kick board or float. Hold the kick board in both hands with arms out straight in front of you. Try not to bare your weight on the kick board at all. Instead relax and allow it to float.

If you find this tricky then you can try the exercise with two kick boards, one held under each arm.

Do not be put off if you feel you are not moving at all. The kick boards provide resistance to the front and therefore they are an excellent way of helping to increase leg kick strength.

After each whip-like leg kick, the feet should then be pointed backwards and inline to provide a streamlined shape as they glide. If the feet remain turned out or toes remain turned up after the legs come together they will cause drag and almost certainly sink.

If possible ensure you submerge your face with each stroke, or at least keep your chin on the water surface and eyes facing forwards and not upwards. This will encourage and flatter and therefore more streamlined body position.

Although breaststroke can be swum with the body at an angle in the water, if the angle is too steep then this results in increased frontal resistance. Combine this with a weak leg kick and you really will go nowhere fast!"

Chapter 16: Butterfly

Basic Butterfly Technique

Butterfly stroke is the most recent stroke, developed in the 1950's, and it is the second fastest stroke to Front Crawl. The stroke evolved from breaststroke as it also contains a simultaneous leg action and simultaneous arm action. The stroke requires a great deal of upper body strength and can be very physically demanding; therefore it is a stroke that is swum competitively rather than recreationally.

Buoyancy is very important because the arms are recovered over the water and the head is raised to breathe, therefore good floaters will achieve this far easier than poor floaters.

The timing and coordination of the stroke is usually a two beat cycle of leg kicks to one arm cycle.

The undulating action of the body and the legs create great demands of the spine, therefore there are many alternative exercises and practices that can be used to make learning the stroke easier and less physical.

Breathing is an explosive exhalation and then inhalation in the short second that the head and face are above the water surface.

The timing and coordination of butterfly is usually a two beat cycle of leg kicks to one arm cycle. One leg kick should have enough power to assist the upper body out and over the water surface and the second leg kick to assist the arms as they recover just over the surface of the water.

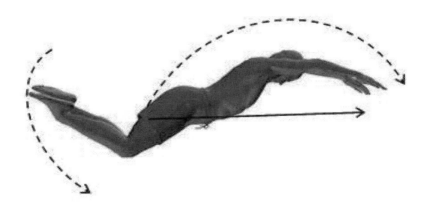

Body Position

The body position varies through the stroke cycle due to the continuous undulating action. The body should undulate from head to toe, producing a dolphin-type action.

Although undulation is unavoidable, the body position should be kept as horizontal as possible to keep frontal resistance to a minimum. Intermittent or alternative breathing will help to maintain this required body position.

The body should be face down (prone) with the crown of the head leading the action.

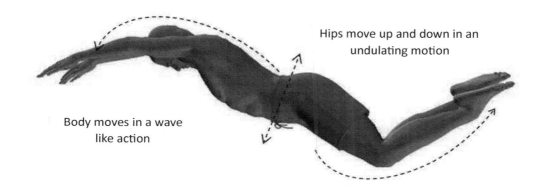

Hips move up and down in an undulating motion

Body moves in a wave like action

The shoulders should remain level throughout and the head should remain central and still, looking down until breathing is required.

Hips should be inline with the shoulders and should remain parallel to the direction of travel.

Common Body Position Mistakes

The most common mistake made when performing the undulating movement is an excessive movement up and down. As the movement originates from the head there is a tendency to over exaggerate this movement, causing the wave movement through the rest of the body to excessive and over pronounced. The swimmer then puts more effort and energy into moving up and down instead of actually swimming forwards.

A simple push and glide exercise from the poolside followed by a gentle undulating movement across the surface of the water helps to eliminate any excessive body movements.
If the swimmer places the effort on using the undulation to move forward then this will provide a solid base from which to build and perfect butterfly stroke.

Leg Kick

The main functions of butterfly stroke leg action are to balance the arm action and help to provide some propulsion. This action then generates the undulating movement of the body position as the swimmer moves through the water.

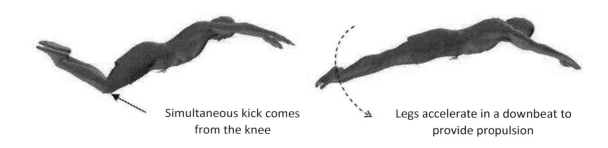

Simultaneous kick comes from the knee

Legs accelerate in a downbeat to provide propulsion

The legs kick simultaneously in an action that is similar to that of front crawl but with a greater and more pronounced knee bend.

The upbeat of the kick should come from the hip and the ankles should be relaxed with toes pointed. The legs move upwards without bending at the knees and the soles of the feet press against the water vertically and backwards.

Knees bend and then straighten on the downbeat to provide propulsion. The legs should accelerate to provide power on the downbeat.

Common Leg Kick Mistakes

A breaststroke type leg kick can sometimes be performed by mistake, due to the simultaneous nature of the kick itself. Most swimmers that are able to perform breaststroke fairly well will naturally kick their legs in a small circle when attempting butterfly leg kick for the first time.

Another common mistake is to place an emphasis on the arm pull for butterfly and therefore lose all power from the leg kick. The legs just go through the motions when in fact they are needed to assist the body to rise out of the water so that the arm pull and recovery can be completed with minimum effort.

A powerful butterfly leg kick is vital and performing the kick whilst holding a float or kickboard out in front with straight arms will help develop the technique and power required for this movement.

Arm Action

Butterfly arm action is a continuous simultaneous movement that requires significant upper body strength. The action of the arms is similar to that of front crawl and the underwater catch, down sweep and upsweep parts draw the shape of a 'keyhole' through its movement path.

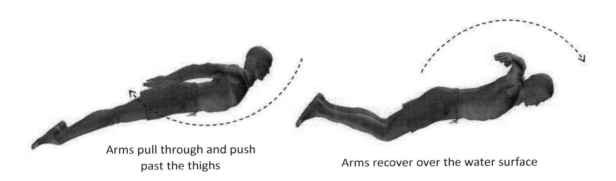

Arms pull through and push
past the thighs

Arms recover over the water surface

Entry

The entry of the hands into the water should be fingertips first, leading with the thumb. Fingers should be together with palms flat and facing outwards. Arms should be stretched forward with a slightly bent elbow. Entry should be with arms extended inline with the shoulders.

Catch and Down Sweep

The pitch of the hands changes to a deeper angle with hands almost vertical. The catch and down sweep should begin just outside the shoulder line. Palms remain facing in the direction of travel. The elbow should bend to about 90 degrees to provide the extra power required. The hands sweep in a circular movement similar to breaststroke, but in a downward path.

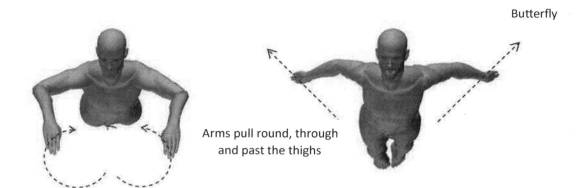

Arms pull round, through
and past the thighs

Upsweep

The pitch of the hands changes to face out and upwards towards the water surface. Elbows extend fully to straighten the arms and hands towards the thighs.

Recovery

Hands and arms must clear the water on recovery in accordance with ASA Law. Arms and hands should exit the water little finger facing upwards. Arms must clear the surface as they are 'thrown' over and forwards. Palms remain facing outwards, naturally giving a thumb-first entry.

Common Arm Pull Mistakes

The two most common mistakes made when it comes to butterfly arm technique are an incomplete or short pull and a wide hand entry.

The arm technique is sometimes compared to front crawl when it is taught to beginners in its most basic form. This is due to the long sweep and the recovery over the water surface. This is where the similarities end and this comparison can sometimes be taken literally, resulting in an almost double front crawl arm action with an excessive elbow bend.

The most common mistake made amongst slightly more advanced butterfly swimmers is a wide hand entry. The hands should enter the water inline with the shoulders. If the entry is wide of the shoulder line then this will result in a weak and inefficient arm pull.

Simply walking though shallow water of about shoulder depth practicing the arm action in slow motion will help to establish a full sweep and an inline hand entry.

Breathing

Breathing technique during butterfly is a rapid and explosive action.

Inhalation takes place as the arms complete their upsweep and begin to recover, as the body begins to rise. The head is lifted enough for the mouth to clear the water and the chin should be pushed forward, but remain at the water surface. Some exhalation underwater takes place during this phase.

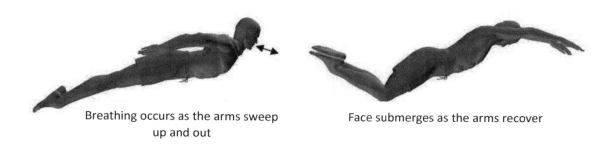

Breathing occurs as the arms sweep up and out

Face submerges as the arms recover

The head is lowered quickly into the water again as the arms recover inline with the shoulders, to resume an overall streamlined position and maintain minimal frontal resistance.

Explosive breathing is normally preferred but a combination of trickle and explosive breathing can be used. Explosive breathing involves a rapid exhalation followed immediately by inhalation, requiring powerful use of the respiratory muscles.

Common Breathing Mistakes

Failure to actually breathe is the most common mistake made by beginners learning butterfly breathing technique.

Because the inhalation and exhalation have to take place very quickly in the short second the face is being raised, it is very common to either inhale only or not breathe at all. The result: a pair of extremely inflated lungs and a severe lack of oxygen.

Performing the full stroke and taking a breath every other stroke cycle is a good way of ensuring that exhalation is taking place and that the lungs are sufficiently emptied before inhalation takes place.

Timing and Coordination

The butterfly stroke cycle should contain 2 leg kicks to 1 arm cycle where the first kick occurs when the arms are forward and the second kick when the have pulled back.

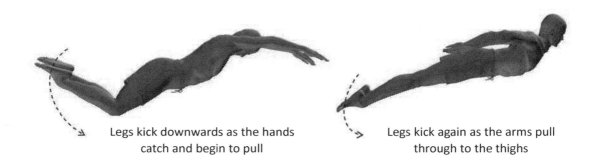

Legs kick downwards as the hands catch and begin to pull

Legs kick again as the arms pull through to the thighs

The downbeat of the first leg kick occurs at the catch and down sweep phase. Both arms will have been in the air during recovery, causing the hips to sink. The subsequent kick should be strong enough to counter balance this hip movement.

The second downbeat leg kick occurs during the powerful and accelerating upsweep phase of the arm cycle. During this movement, the feet react towards the hands and the strength will contribute towards propulsion.

Breathing can occur every stroke cycle or every other stroke cycle, but should not interrupt the flow of the leg kick and arm pull timing cycles.

A simple breakdown of the arm pull and leg kick coordination for butterfly is:

Kick - Pull - Kick - Recover

Common Timing Mistakes

Timing and coordination issues can occur when the swimmer attempts to kick and pull at the same time. There should be a delay from the leg kick as the arms pull, so that the first powerful leg kick assists the arms recovery.

Beginners learning butterfly tend to miss out the second supporting leg kick as the arms recover.

A good way to practice and develop the timing for this stroke is to swim using a butterfly leg kick and a breaststroke arm pull. There is less energy used when swimming with breaststroke arms because the arms recover under the water surface.

Therefore it is an ideal way to ensure that there are two leg kicks for each arm pull, where one leg kick assists the body to rise and breathe, and the other smaller leg kick assists the arms to recover.

Once this exercise is perfected then the swimmer can reintroduce butterfly arms into the stroke and maintain the timing and coordination pattern.

Full Stroke Overview

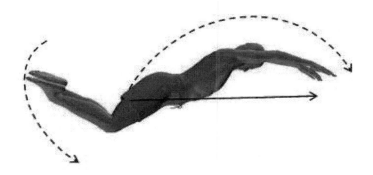

Legs kick downwards as the arms begin to pull. The legs kick again as the arms complete their pull and recover over the water. Breathing occurs every stroke or every second stroke cycle.

Butterfly Exercises

The next section contains practical exercises to help learn and fine-tune each separate part of your butterfly technique.

They are designed to isolate each element of the stroke so that you can learn exactly what each part of your body should be doing.

BUTTERFLY: Body Position

Holding the poolside

Aim: to practise the body position and movement by holding on to the poolside.

The swimmer performs an undulating action whilst using the poolside or rail for support. Note: this exercise should be performed slowly and without force or power as the static nature places pressure on the lower back.

Key Actions

- Keep your head in the middle
- Make the top of your head lead first
- Keep your shoulders level
- Keep your hips level
- Make your body into a long wave

Technical Focus

- Exercise should be slow and gradual

- Head remains central

- Shoulders and hips should be level

- Horizontal body with an undulating movement

- Wave like movement from head to toe

- Legs remain together

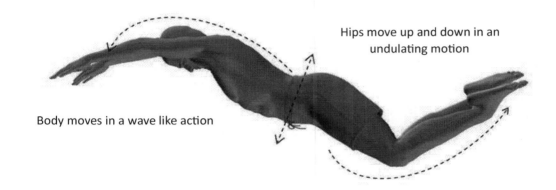

Hips move up and down in an undulating motion

Body moves in a wave like action

Common Faults

- Body remains too stiff and rigid

- Head moves to the sides

- Shoulders and hips are not remaining level

BUTTERFLY: Body Position

Dolphin dives

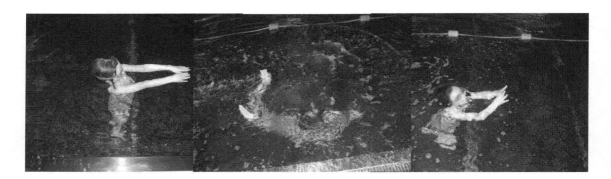

Aim: to develop an undulating body movement whilst travelling through water of standing depth.

The swimmer performs a series of dives from a standing position, diving deep under the surface, arching the back and resurfacing immediately to stand up. The aim is to perform as many dolphin dives across the width as possible. Swimmers can then progress to performing the practice without standing in-between dives.

Key Actions

- Keep your head in the middle
- Make the top of your head dive down first
- Make your body into a huge wave
- Stretch up to the surface

Technical Focus

- Head remains central

- Shoulders and hips should be level

- Body moves with an undulating movement

- Wave-like movement from head to toe

- Legs remain together

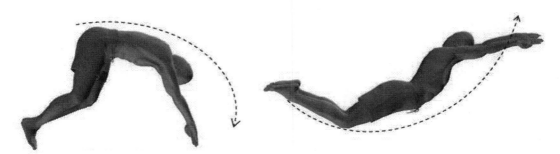

Body dives down and then resurfaces immediately in a wave like movement

Common Faults

- Body remains too stiff and rigid

- Body dives but fails to undulate upwards

- Leading with the head looking forwards

BUTTERFLY: Body Position

Push and glide

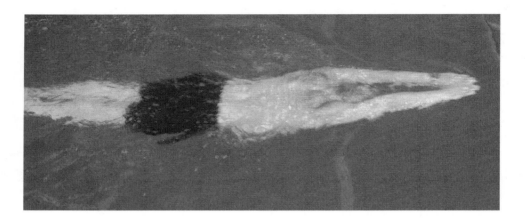

Aim: to practise and develop an undulating action whilst moving.

The swimmer pushes from the poolside into a glide and then begins the undulating action from head to toe. This allows the swimmer to experience the required undulating action whilst moving through the water.

Key Actions

- Make the top of your head lead first
- Keep your shoulders level
- Keep your hips level
- Make your body into a long wave
- Pretend you are a dolphin swimming

Technical Focus

- Head remains central
- Shoulders and hips should be level
- Body is horizontal with an undulating movement
- Wave-like movement from head to toe
- Legs remain together

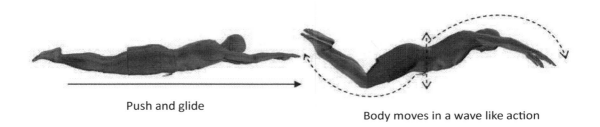

Push and glide

Body moves in a wave like action

Common Faults

- Body remains too stiff and rigid
- Shoulders and hips are not remaining level
- Leading with the head looking forwards

BUTTERFLY: Legs

Sitting on the poolside

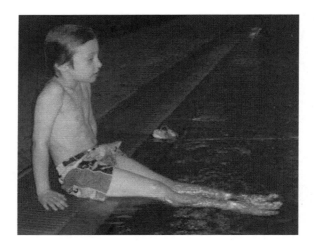

Aim: to develop the kicking action whilst sitting on the poolside.

Bending and kicking from the knees with legs together allows the swimmer to practise the correct movement and feel the water at the same time.

Key Actions

- Kick both legs at the same time
- Keep your ankles loose
- Keep your legs together
- Point your toes

Technical Focus

- Simultaneous legs action
- Knees bend and kick in upbeat to provide propulsion
- Legs accelerate on upbeat
- Toes are pointed

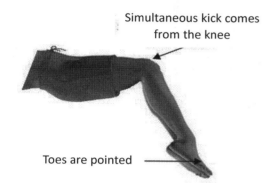

Simultaneous kick comes from the knee

Toes are pointed

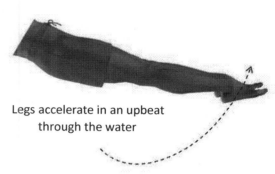

Legs accelerate in an upbeat through the water

Common Faults

- Leg kick is not simultaneous
- Toes are not pointed
- Overall action is too stiff and rigid
- Kick is not deep or powerful enough

BUTTERFLY: Legs

Push and glide adding leg kick

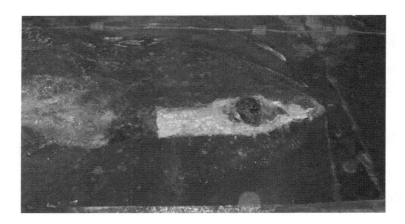

Aim: to practise the dolphin leg kick action and experience movement.

This allows the swimmer the develop propulsion from the accelerating leg kick and undulating body movement.

Key Actions

- Keep your ankles loose
- Kick downwards powerfully
- Keep your legs together
- Point your toes
- Kick like a mermaid

Technical Focus

- Simultaneous legs action
- Knees bend and kick in downbeat to provide propulsion
- Legs accelerate on downbeat
- Toes are pointed
- Hips initiate undulating movement

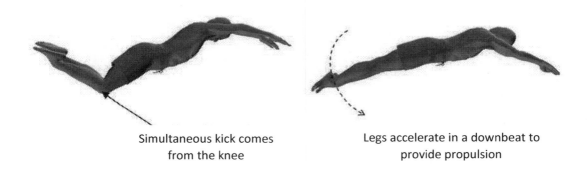

Simultaneous kick comes
from the knee

Legs accelerate in a downbeat to
provide propulsion

Common Faults

- Leg kick is not simultaneous
- Toes are not pointed
- Overall action is too stiff and rigid
- Kick is not deep or powerful enough

BUTTERFLY: Legs

Prone holding a float with both hands

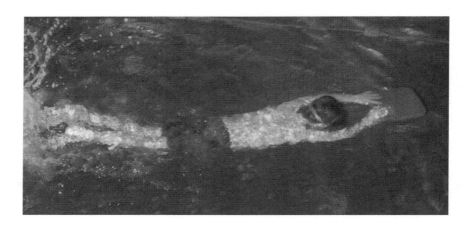

Aim: to develop the leg kick using a float for support.

This practice allows the advanced swimmer to develop leg kick strength and stamina as the float isolates the legs.

Key Actions

- Kick with both legs at the same time
- Kick downwards powerfully
- Keep your legs together
- Create a wave-like action through your body
- Kick like a mermaid

Technical Focus

- Simultaneous legs action

- Knees bend and kick in downbeat to provide propulsion

- Legs accelerate on downbeat

- Toes are pointed

- Hips initiate undulating movement

Powerful leg kick provides propulsion and helps the body to undulate

Common Faults

- Leg kick is not simultaneous

- Toes are not pointed

- Overall action is too stiff and rigid

- Kick is not deep or powerful enough

BUTTERFLY: Legs

Supine position with arms by sides

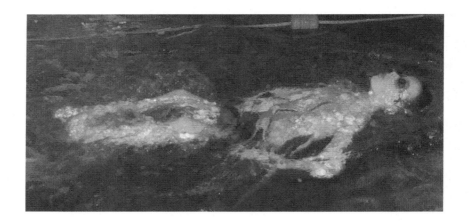

Aim: to practise and develop a dolphin leg kick action in a supine position.

This allows the swimmer to kick continuously whilst facing upwards. This practice requires a great deal of leg strength and stamina and therefore is ideal for developing these aspects of the stroke.

Key Actions

- Kick both legs at the same time
- Keep your ankles loose
- Kick upwards powerfully
- Keep your legs together
- Point your toes

Technical Focus

- Simultaneous legs action
- Knees bend and kick in upbeat to provide propulsion
- Legs accelerate on upbeat
- Toes are pointed
- Hips initiate undulating movement

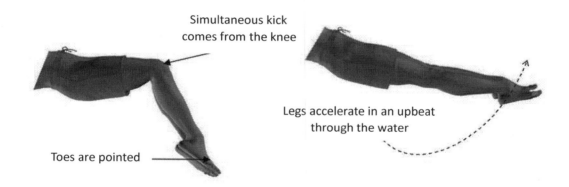

Simultaneous kick comes from the knee

Legs accelerate in an upbeat through the water

Toes are pointed

Common Faults

- Leg kick is not simultaneous
- Overall action is too stiff and rigid
- Hips are not undulating to initiate the kick
- Kick is not deep or powerful enough

BUTTERFLY: Legs

Kick and roll

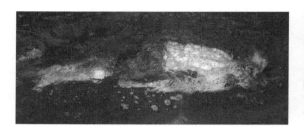 

Aim: to combine the leg kick and undulating body movement and perform a rolling motion through the water.

This practice can be performed with arms held by the sides or held out in front. The rolling motion forces the swimmer to use the head, shoulders and hips to produce the movement required for powerful undulating propulsion.

Key Actions

- Kick both legs at the same time
- Keep your ankles loose
- Roll like a corkscrew
- Keep your legs together
- Make your body snake through the water

Technical Focus

- Simultaneous legs action

- Head and shoulders initiate rolling motion

- Knees bend and kick to provide propulsion

- Legs accelerate on downbeat

- Hips initiate undulating movement

Legs kick as the body performs a 'cork screw' like roll through the water

Common Faults

- Leg kick is not simultaneous

- Overall action is too stiff and rigid

- Kick is not powerful enough

BUTTERFLY: Arms

Standing on the poolside

Aim: to practise correct butterfly arm action whilst standing on the poolside.

The pupil is able to work through the arm action slowly and in stages so as to experience the basic movement required.

Key Actions

- Move both arms at the same time
- Thumbs go in first
- Draw a keyhole under your body
- Push past your thighs

Technical Focus

- Arms move simultaneously

- Hands enter the water in line with the shoulders

- Hands pull in the shape of a keyhole

- Hands push past the thigh

Arms pull through in a keyhole shape

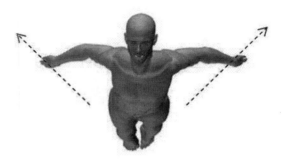

Arms pull through and past the thighs

Common Faults

- Arm action is not simultaneous

- Arms are too straight

- Arms are not pulling back to the thighs

BUTTERFLY: Arms

Walking on the pool floor

Aim: to progress from the previous practice and develop the arm action.

The swimmer can get a feel for the water whilst walking and performing the simultaneous arm action.

Key Actions

- Move both arms at the same time
- Thumbs go in first
- Draw a keyhole under your body
- Push past your thighs

Technical Focus

- Arms move simultaneously

- Hands enter the water in line with the shoulders

- Hands pull in the shape of a keyhole

- Hands push past the thigh

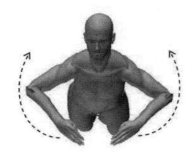

Arms pull through simultaneously

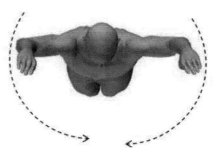

Arms are thrown forwards over the water surface

Common Faults

- Arm action is not simultaneous

- Arms are too straight

- Fingers are apart

- Hands fail to clear the water

BUTTERFLY: Arms

Push and glide adding arms

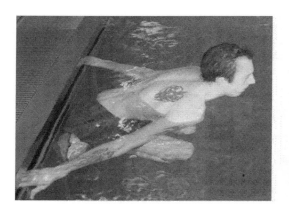 

Aim: to practise the arm action whilst moving through the water.

Correct body position is established from the push and glide and the swimmer can then use the arm action to maintain momentum through the water. A limited number of arm pulls can be achieved with this practice.

Key Actions

- Move both arms at the same time
- Thumbs enter water first
- Pull hard through the water
- Pull past your thighs
- Throw your arms over the water

Technical Focus

- Arms move simultaneously

- Fingers closed together

- Thumbs enter the water first

- Hands enter the water in line with the shoulders

- Hands push past the thigh

- Hands clear water surface on recovery

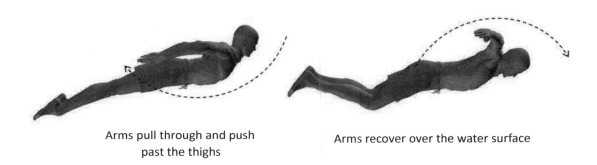

Arms pull through and push
past the thighs

Arms recover over the water surface

Common Faults

- Arms are too straight

- Arms are not pulling back to the thighs

- Hands fail to clear the water

BUTTERFLY: Arms

Arms only using a pull-buoy

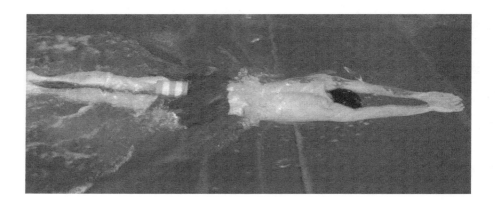

Aim: to help the swimmer develop arm strength and stamina.

This practice is performed over a longer distance, progressing from the previous practice. The pull buoy provides buoyancy and support as well as helps the undulating body movement.

Key Actions

- Thumbs go in first
- Pull hard through the water
- Pull past your thighs
- Throw your arms over the water

Technical Focus

- Arms move simultaneously
- Fingers closed together
- Thumbs enter the water first
- Hands enter the water in line with the shoulders
- Hands push past the thigh
- Hands clear water surface on recovery

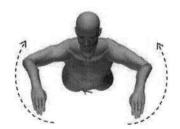

Arms pull though the water with power

Hands and arms clear the water on recovery

Common Faults

- Arms are too straight
- Arms are not pulling back to the thighs
- Hands fail to clear the water

BUTTERFLY: Arms

Arm action with breaststroke leg kicks

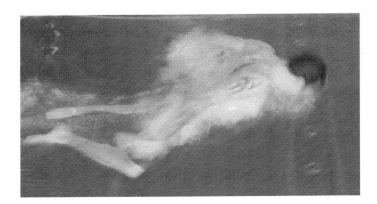

Aim: to enable use of breaststroke leg kicks to support the arm action.

As the legs kick, the propulsion helps the body to rise and the arms to recover over the water surface. This practice is also a good introduction to the timing of butterfly arms and legs.

Key Actions

- Thumbs go in first
- Draw a keyhole under your body
- Pull past your thighs
- Little finger comes out first
- Throw your arms over the water

Technical Focus

- Thumbs enter the water first

- Hands pull in the shape of a keyhole

- Hands push past the thigh

- Little finger exits the water first

- Hands clear water surface on recovery

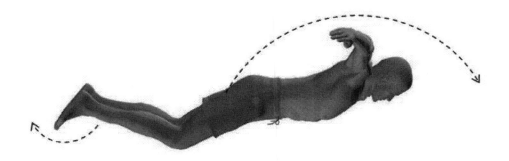

Legs kick to help to arms recover over the water surface

Common Faults

- Arms are too straight

- Arms are not pulling back to the thighs

- Fingers are apart

- Hands fail to clear the water

BUTTERFLY: Breathing

Standing breathing, with arm pulls

Aim: to incorporate butterfly breathing into the arm action.

This practice is performed standing either on the poolside or stationary in water of standing depth.

Key Actions

- Blow out hard as your chin rises
- Put your face down as your arms recover
- Push your chin forward and breathe every arm pull or every two arm pulls

Technical Focus

- Breathing in should occur as the arms sweep up and out

- Explosive breathing is most beneficial

- Chin should remain in the water

- Face dives into the water as the arms come level with the shoulders

- Breath can be taken every stroke cycle or alternate cycles

Breathing occurs as the arms sweep
up and out

Face submerges as the arms recover

Common Faults

- Lifting the head too high

- Arms stop recovery to breathe

- Holding the breath

BUTTERFLY: Breathing

Full stroke

Aim: to use the full stroke to practice breathing, incorporating regular breaths into the arm and leg actions.

Key Actions

- Blow out hard as your chin rises
- Lift your head to breathe in as your legs kick down
- Put your face down as your arms come over
- Push your chin forward and breathe every arm pull or every two arm pulls

Technical Focus

- Breathing in occurs as the arms sweep upwards
- Breathing in occurs as the legs are kicking downwards
- Explosive breathing is most beneficial
- Chin remains in the water
- Face dives into the water as the arms come level with the shoulders
- Breath can be taken every stroke cycle or alternate cycles

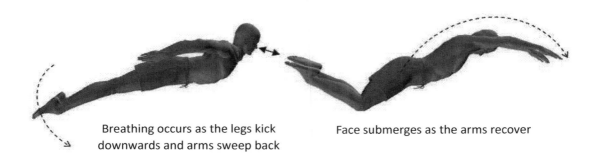

Breathing occurs as the legs kick downwards and arms sweep back

Face submerges as the arms recover

Common Faults

- Lifting the head too high
- Arms stop recovery to breathe
- Holding the breath
- Breathing too often

BUTTERFLY: Timing

Full stroke

Aim: to perform the full stroke butterfly, incorporating two leg kicks per arm pull.

Key Actions

- Kick hard as your hands enter the water
- Kick again as your hands pull under your body

Technical Focus

- Two legs kicks per arm cycle
- Legs kick once as hands enter and sweep out
- Legs kick once as arms sweep up and out

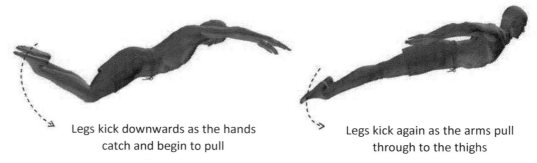

Legs kick downwards as the hands catch and begin to pull

Legs kick again as the arms pull through to the thighs

Common Faults

- Only kicking once per arm cycle
- Kicking too many times per arm cycle

"Now that you have finished my book, would you please consider writing a review? Reviews are the best way readers discover great new books. I would truly appreciate it."

Mark Young

For more information about learning to swim and improving your swimming strokes and swimming technique visit **Swim Teach**.

"The number one resource for learning to swim
and improving swimming technique."
www.swim-teach.com

More books by Mark Young:

How To Be A Swimming Teacher
The Definitive Guide To Becoming A Successful Swimming Teacher

The Complete Guide To Simple Swimming
Everything You Need to Know from Your First Entry into the Pool to Swimming the Four Basic Strokes

The Swimming Strokes Book:
82 Easy Exercises For Learning How To Swim The Four Basic Swimming Strokes

How To Swim Front Crawl
A Step-By-Step Guide For Beginners Learning Front Crawl Technique

How To Swim Breaststroke
A Step-By-Step Guide For Beginners Learning Breaststroke Technique

How To Swim Backstroke
A Step-By-Step Guide For Beginners Learning Backstroke Technique

How To Swim Butterfly
A Step-By-Step Guide For Beginners Learning Butterfly Technique

Made in the USA
Columbia, SC
07 June 2024

36693639R00154